Narcissism

Delve Into The Underlying Causes Of The Disorder, And Strengthen Your Defenses Against Narcissistic Influence And Manipulation

(The Exhaustive Manual On Overcoming Narcissism)

Christian Ethier

TABLE OF CONTENT

What Is A Narcissist? 1

Communicating With A Narcissist 19

Understanding Narcissism 33

Eft Tapping 75

Narcissist In A Relationship 90

The Impact Of Narcissistic Abuse On Affected Individuals 101

Ensuring Self-Preservation Against A Manipulative Relative Engaging In Gaslighting 117

Indicators Of Interacting With An Individual Displaying Narcissistic Traits 139

What Is A Narcissist?

Each of us is acquainted with individuals who exude immense self-assurance and hold a lofty opinion of themselves. However, despite their lack of pleasantness, these individuals exhibit a pronounced tendency towards egocentrism, even if they are capable of maintaining a moderately conventional lifestyle. In contrast, individuals with narcissistic tendencies encounter numerous challenges across various domains of their lives, encompassing but not limited to their professional endeavors, interpersonal connections, and financial matters. Consequently, what delineates an individual who is primarily focused on themselves from someone exhibiting traits of pathological self-absorption commonly termed as narcissism? Why is it that one individual is able to lead a conventional lifestyle, while the other grapples with adversity?

To begin with, it is important to recognize that narcissism is a personality disorder that does not arise innately but rather emerges gradually under specific circumstances. An individual afflicted with narcissistic personality disorder is characterized by an inherent craving for recognition, an exaggerated perception of their own significance veiling vulnerable self-regard, and, arguably the most prominent trait, an utter absence of empathy towards others. Empathy is a fundamental characteristic inherent to human nature that fosters the ability to comprehend and connect with the emotions of others. Lacking empathy prohibits the establishment of genuine interpersonal connections. This is the reason why individuals with narcissistic traits are incapable of forming healthy relationships, whether they be of a romantic nature or pertaining to other aspects of life.

Based on the findings presented in a scholarly article featured in the Journal of Clinical Psychiatry, it is discerned that narcissistic personality disorder (NPD) manifests in approximately 7.7% of males and 4.8% of females over the course of their lives. Furthermore, the research conducted by Nordqvist (2018) revealed that individuals belonging to the young adult demographic, those who have experienced divorce or separation from their partner, and individuals from racial minority groups exhibited elevated likelihoods of developing narcissistic tendencies. Based on our analysis, it can be inferred that under the appropriate circumstances, individuals of any gender, race, or age have the potential to develop narcissistic tendencies. This finding challenges the prevailing notion that narcissism is exclusively associated with males.

Now, let us proceed to delve deeper into the characteristics exhibited by individuals with narcissistic tendencies, in order to comprehensively grasp the extent of this specific personality disorder. By the conclusion of this chapter, we will discern its unique qualities in comparison to other widely recognized personality disorders, such as psychopathy and sociopathy.

An inflated perception of one's own significance.

The sense of self-importance that is experienced by a narcissist diverges from both vanity and excessive confidence. The most suitable term to define it would be "grandiosity," which encompasses an inflated perception of superiority founded on unrealistic grounds. Narcissistic individuals hold the perception that they possess exceptional qualities and harbor a desire to affiliate with individuals, locations, or circumstances that hold high regard, as they perceive themselves as surpassing ordinary or standard attributes. This perception of superiority is frequently constructed internally, independent of tangible accomplishments in real-world settings. They will anticipate others to afford them a sense of superiority and, in order to achieve this, they will resort to misrepresenting their skills and accomplishments while consistently projecting themselves as the more virtuous individual in any given circumstance, whether it pertains to personal relationships or professional pursuits.

In summary, a narcissist assumes the role of an individual of superior standing, encompassing all spheres of life, and will employ any means necessary to uphold this position, such as engaging in deceit, distorting the truth, and belittling others.

The persistent requirement for acknowledgment and validation

Although they promote a feeling of superiority, they possess a certain level of awareness regarding the illusory nature of it. This is the reason they require consistent commendation and acknowledgment to sustain the façade. Compliments alone do not suffice for individuals with narcissistic tendencies. They will actively search for individuals who will provide them with consistent validation, and who will attend to their needs tirelessly, without reciprocating anything in return. They anticipate that those in their vicinity will regard them with utmost admiration, and even the most subtle criticisms will be perceived as a direct affront, leading the narcissist to engage in abusive behavior.

A narcissist's relationships are inherently asymmetrical. They display an excessive preoccupation with themselves and lack the ability to empathize with their partner, compromising their comprehension of their partner's emotions and sentiments.

Entitlement

Despite their lack of deservingness, a narcissist will display an abnormal sense of entitlement towards luxuries and privileges. They shall have the anticipation that individuals shall conduct themselves in a specific manner and perpetually be available for their service. Individuals who fail to adhere to this expectation will encounter various levels of hostility, potentially resulting in complete exclusion from the narcissist's social circle. They hold the conviction that they are deserving of all they desire, and they exhibit no apprehension in demonstrating this belief.

Taking advantage of the individuals in their existence.

As previously mentioned in the introductory section of this chapter, narcissists possess an inherent inability to experience empathy, akin to a void or vacuous entity. In the case of a narcissist, the individuals in their social sphere are regarded more as mere instruments and commodities, serving as a means to achieve their own objectives, rather than being recognized as genuine human entities. They employ any means necessary to fulfill their personal desires, utilizing and taking advantage of the individuals within their sphere, with a notable absence of remorse, guilt, or shame. This is the reason why it is highly perilous to have an individual with narcissistic tendencies in one's personal sphere. Comprehending the inability of an individual to experience empathy, remorse, or guilt poses a considerable challenge, considering these emotional states are typically universal among the majority of individuals, and it is commonly assumed that all human beings possess them.

Individuals with narcissistic tendencies exhibit a lack of moral constraint when it comes to exploiting others in various circumstances, as long as it serves their personal interests, while consistently evading accountability for any harm they may inflict upon others. They will persist in utilizing evasive tactics, refusing to provide thorough answers or accept accountability, effectively resembling an immovable barrier, until you find yourself in a state of perplexion and compliance. The entirety of the relationships they form stem from their respective requirements. Frequently, they will make certain to secure the assistance of multiple individuals to attend to their various requirements, encompassing areas such as accommodation, financial support, physical intimacy, or other forms of assistance.

Residing within a realm of one's imagination

A narcissistic individual possesses a profoundly tenuous connection with the objective realm of existence. The individual exhibits a predilection for dwelling within a self-constructed realm of imagination, wherein they possess the ability to portray an idealized version of themselves while disregarding any unsupportive elements. They are consciously deceiving themselves in order to safeguard the sense of superiority that is harmful to their survival, while suppressing any contradictions or facts that contradict their distorted reasoning. Due to their inherent feelings of insecurity, this envisioned realm serves as their coping mechanism for confronting the disappointing aspects of their actual existence. It enables them to derive satisfaction from a distorted perception of achievement, notoriety, and social acceptance, while their protective mechanisms respond strongly in the face of any potential encroachment or exposure of their false reality.

Engaging in denigration of others in order to elevate oneself

The narcissist's inner core becomes unsettled by individuals who possess attributes or accomplishments that they themselves lack, including financial resources, achievements, or simply the admiration and esteem of others. They will employ all possible tactics, such as condescension, insulting remarks, bullying, and any other strategies at their disposal, to undermine individuals who pose a threat to their sense of self-importance, with the intention of eroding their self-esteem. Regardless of the harm they may cause, narcissists are solely focused on maintaining their personal delusions and exhibit a complete lack of remorse or accountability for their conduct.

Monopolizing

Engaging in a dialogue with a narcissist is akin to observing a television program. They have a strong desire to be in the spotlight, and they will go to great lengths to assert their dominance, even if it results in interrupting or disregarding the input of others. Their self-centeredness demands that everything revolves around them, regardless of the circumstances, and their emotions of envy become apparent whenever they are not the center of attention.

In the presence of a narcissist, all facets of interaction become unilaterally oriented, encompassing relationships, conversations, and various circumstances. Due to their exclusive self-interest, their concerns are only relevant if they can exploit them for personal gain.

Unstable mood

Upon realizing the divergence between their imagined ideal self and their real identity, narcissists will exhibit a diverse array of emotions. They will experience a sense of vulnerability and sadness, and may even encounter episodes of depression. Furthermore, owing to their limited capacity to confront actuality, they struggle to assimilate changes or unfamiliar circumstances and exhibit inadequate stress management skills. In their final attempts to safeguard their ego, individuals with narcissistic tendencies may resort to targeted aggression against those in their vicinity, employing abuse as a means to restore their desired sense of superiority and control. They will not yield to any circumstances that would compromise the preservation of their illusion. The narcissist's combination of fragility and absence of empathy, remorse, and guilt renders them a detrimental and abusive presence in any relationship, irrespective of the sincere efforts made by the other party to cater to their needs.

There is significant bewilderment surrounding three widely recognized forms of personality disorders, namely narcissism, psychopathy, and sociopathy. What distinguishes them from one another? How can we ascertain the nature of the matter at hand?

Psychopathy and sociopathy are regarded as distinct manifestations of a specific class of personality disorders known as antisocial personality disorders. They exhibit numerous characteristics including duplicity, hostility, irritability, a proclivity for engaging in unlawful behavior, a deficiency in displaying remorse or empathy, and an inability to assume accountability for their actions.

One distinguishing factor right from the outset is that psychopaths are innately predisposed, whereas sociopaths are shaped by their environment. What does that mean? There is a consensus among experts that psychopathy primarily arises from impaired development in the regions of the brain responsible for regulating emotions and restraining impulsive behavior, notwithstanding the role played by environmental factors, traumatic experiences, and various forms of abuse on both conditions. Psychopaths exhibit a deficient capacity for emotions and a limited ability to comprehend emotional reactions since their early stages of development, whereas sociopaths are a product of traumatic experiences and may acquire this disorder at any point in their lifetime. The prevalence of sociopathy is significantly elevated. Based on statistical data, it can be observed that approximately 4% of the United States population possesses sociopathic tendencies, a rather somber reality.

Narcissists exhibit certain characteristics akin to these antisocial disorders, such as deficient empathy and an exaggerated self-conception. Nevertheless, they typically do not manifest physical aggressiveness, nor do they display impulsivity. The aggressive behavior displayed by a narcissist typically manifests through verbal abuse and manipulation, with physical confrontation being a comparatively infrequent occurrence. Their longing for admiration from others, and thus their reliance on the attention of others, distinguishes them from the realm of antisocial personality disorders. Between the two options, it can be argued that narcissism bears a greater resemblance to sociopathy due to its multifactorial origins, rather than being solely attributable to underdeveloped brain functions. The narcissist's inclination towards a pursuit of "perfection" is the primary factor that reduces their likelihood of engaging in criminal behavior, thereby distinguishing them significantly from the inherently destructive sociopath.

Having a comprehensive understanding of the characteristics and behaviors associated with narcissism is of utmost importance in order to gain insights into the individual with whom you have or have had a close relationship. Furthermore, this knowledge is essential in effectively detaching oneself from their influence and ultimately achieving liberation. Please bear in mind that due to their marked absence of empathy, establishing a mutually beneficial relationship with them proves unattainable. Hence, it is important to acknowledge that the failure of the relationship is not attributable to any shortcomings on your part. You are entitled to experience happiness and receive love, just like any other individual in this world; therefore, do not harbor any remorse about distancing yourself from a narcissistic individual.

Communicating With A Narcissist

As individuals, we are perpetually engaged in ongoing communication with both ourselves and others. Empathy plays a pivotal role in facilitating exceptional communication. However, what transpires when you seek to engage with an individual who lacks the capacity for empathy? Engaging in dialogue with an individual afflicted with narcissism can be exceedingly formidable and mentally taxing. It often manifests as an unidirectional discourse that is orchestrated by the individuals in question. Communicating with individuals who exhibit narcissistic traits may present a challenge in effectively conveying one's ideas, emotions, and explanations.

"When faced with apparent incffcctivcncss in communicating with a narcissistic individual, consider employing the following communication strategies specifically tailored to narcissistic traits:

Please refrain from responding based on emotions.

Engaging in narcissistic behavior can be damaging and appear as excessive attacks on one's personal being. However, it must be noted that narcissism does not exhibit selective tendencies; its conceited behaviors and attitudes have a tendency to manifest in every one of their interpersonal connections.

Having an awareness that these harmful tendencies stem from their fears could potentially render it more tolerable to refrain from resorting to violence and elevate the level of conversation. It is imperative to allocate sufficient time to respond in order to mitigate the escalation of contentious exchanges.

Paraphrasing what's being expressed:

Fundamentally, Narcissistic Personality Disorder entails an insatiable yearning for enduring adulation. In light of the need for acknowledgement, it is imperative to exhibit attentiveness and actively demonstrate receptivity and engagement Utilizing techniques of paraphrasing can be a highly effective method to convey this information, while simultaneously providing the speaker with the opportunity to hear their own thoughts. Example: "It is of utmost importance to me that I attain a thorough comprehension of your perspective." The impression I am getting from your words is that you believe I have caused harm to you in some manner.

Employ the PCC strategy (praise, confront, and compliment) to address the matter: Narcissistic individuals acquire an exceedingly unfavorable standing, which can be understood given their objectionable interpersonal behaviors. The act of shaming and deriding will not serve to rectify or enhance the issue at hand. Utilizing a strategy that I have termed the PCC approach could potentially aid in aligning your needs with their own. Commence by showering commendations, subsequent to which convey the intended message and culminate the discourse with a compliment. This approach aligns with the narcissist's inclination to seek admiration while concurrently granting you the opportunity for self-expression.

Maintain concise conversations: When engaging with an individual displaying narcissistic traits, it is advisable to limit interactions to brief exchanges. Individuals with narcissistic traits exhibit deficiencies in their interpersonal abilities, making it challenging to establish and navigate close relationships, often demonstrating a notable absence of empathy. Protracting the communication process has a tendency to facilitate the emergence of such limitations.

It is of paramount importance to ensure authenticity and sincerity towards oneself. Nevertheless, engaging in conversation with a narcissist can prove to be exceedingly challenging. The narcissistic tendencies of individuals often drive them to engage in behaviors they would not typically undertake. This is precisely why upholding impartiality during discussions is of utmost importance.

Instances of impartial perspectives encompass;

I appreciate you sharing that information.

I will need to consider the matter and provide you with a response at a later time.

I understand and acknowledge your perspective.

It is evident that your belief lies in that statement.

Addressing Uncomfortable Discourse with an Individual Exhibiting Narcissistic Traits

Addressing an individual exhibiting narcissistic traits or suffering from Narcissistic Personality Disorder can be disagreeable, but it may become imperative to assert oneself. Should you wish to engage with a narcissist, it does not necessarily equate to engaging in conflict or contention. Engaging in confrontation could be viewed as

effectively and tactfully expressing oneself. It may also seem as if you are imposing personal boundaries to protect your thoughts, feelings, and physical well-being. The primary apprehension of an individual with narcissistic tendencies often revolves around the perception of being vulnerable. Given this information, endeavor to refrain from
Internalizing the remarks or assertions made by an individual exhibiting abusive behavior. Do these instead;

Exhibit conviction: Recognize your inherent worth and unwaveringly uphold that position. Make an effort to refrain from appearing passive, as individuals with narcissistic traits often interpret passivity as a sign of vulnerability.

Remain composed: Endeavor to refrain from reacting or engaging in conflict, even in the event that the narcissist does so.

Proposal: Endeavor to maintain your strategic approach and objectives in mind. Prior to commencing a discussion, it would be advantageous to acquire a comprehensive understanding of several key aspects: your specific objectives, the potential motives of the narcissist, your own constraints, and the extent of your influence within the relationship.

Acquire Understanding of NPD: Obtaining knowledge regarding NPD and narcissistic tendencies can enhance your comprehension of narcissistic abuse and the condition as a whole.

Distinguish between the activity and the individual: When indicating an issue, make an effort to respect your preferences by utilizing "I" statements that address the actions of others. This can serve as a gentle reminder to the individual with narcissistic tendencies about the boundaries and limitations that they may have exceeded and the level of treatment that you are willing to accept.

Why are Narcs Sex-addicts?

I have carefully pondered these questions multiple times within the recesses of my thoughts, until a singular moment arrived when I experienced a sudden enlightenment, a moment of profound realization.
Upon scrutinizing the accounts of those who have fallen victim to narcissists, a recurring pattern emerges whereby identical inquiries and assertions are raised on multiple occasions.

Inquiries such as: what is the reason behind their intense preoccupation with matters related to sexuality? Detail the numerous extramarital relationships they engaged in and elucidate the accompanying conduct devoid of any expression of remorse or apology, leaving only an empty expression on their visage. We consistently find this appearance exceedingly unsettling. The frequency associated with sexual energy is the most elevated among all others. Notably, it holds a higher position in terms of frequency even when compared to love.

A person suffering from narcissism is fully committed to pursuing their sexual desires, regardless of the consequences, even if it means defying societal norms or moral boundaries and going to great lengths to satisfy those cravings. He does so for a compelling justification.

He possesses no knowledge of love and has never experienced its presence in his lifetime. We ought to acknowledge our fortune, for we possess the capacity to experience love, compassion, and profound emotional upheaval, even when confronted with the distressing sight of a blameless individual, regardless of age or gender, being ruthlessly slain before our eyes on the television. The distressing nature of the visuals could potentially result in insomnia as a consequence of post-traumatic stress.

For the typical individual with typical neurological development, sexual matters hold significance but they do not constitute the entirety of their existence.

We acknowledge its sanctity due to its pivotal role in the perpetuation of the human species.

However, when examined in isolation from an intimate partnership, the body inherently oscillates at a heightened frequency for a duration of several minutes. Romantic relationships between individuals of the same gender possess the ability to transcend all societal obstacles.

Please appreciate that the individual devoid of empathy, known as a narcissist, is compelled to rely heavily on sexual encounters to momentarily capture a fraction of the affectionate emotions that we commonly associate with love. Merely gazing into his eyes reveals a profound sense of powerlessness.

This represents the sole approach to endeavor towards attaining the provision of affection. For him, it resembles a transient armada as, lacking the vessel known as soul that can perpetually embrace love, it eludes him on each occasion.

Ladies and gentlemen, regrettably, this is the most disheartening aspect of the situation. It is truly disheartening that you are now gaining insight into the reasons why certain individuals choose to remain. Why do certain individuals invest years in repairing them, akin to how one mends a child's broken toy?

Occasionally, there are moments when you also perceive the potential for him to develop affection. Take another moment to consider his gaze, filled with yearning, in which he briefly beholds you not as a mere mortal being, but as an ethereal being of divine purity. He perceives a newfound glimmer of hope, as if a savior has emerged to absolve his weary spirit. Despite your perceived potential, you too have proven to be unsuccessful in meeting his expectations. Therefore, kindly allow him to continue his reckless pursuit of promiscuity without concern for the sources from which he acquires his indulgences.

Engaging in sexual activities provides a brief insight for an individual with narcissistic tendencies into the type of intimate affection that they fundamentally lack the capacity to genuinely experience or possess.

He persists in inflicting punishment upon the individual in his immediate proximity; if only he could extract her essence and implant it within his vacant being. Despite his attempt at imitation, it diminishes swiftly.

He has no choice but to inflict cruelty, mental torment, and devaluation upon her in order to completely erode her spirit.

Understanding Narcissism

WHAT IS NARCISSISM?

The term "narcissism" originates from the Greek mythological tale of Narcissus, an exquisite young man who becomes infatuated with his own likeness as seen in a reflection. Narcissistic individuals are those who possess an inflated perception of their own value and importance.

Numerous individuals with narcissistic tendencies, for instance, exhibit an exaggerated sense of self-assurance regarding their abilities or achievements. Certain individuals are preoccupied with their physical appearance. Certain individuals desire authority or sway. Narcissists typically deem themselves to possess exceptional qualities when compared to others. Irrespective of their actual social standing, they perceive themselves as highly significant individuals and aspire to be perceived in a similar light by others. They derive satisfaction and fulfillment from the accolades and admiration bestowed upon them by others.

Nevertheless, their sense of superiority rapidly gives way to humbleness when confronted with critique from others. When such an event occurs, it typically leads to extreme anger, refusal, or an onslaught of derogatory remarks. The aforementioned comments are skillfully expressed in order to assertively establish the offender's proper position. The cumulative effect of these various activities has resulted in a decrease in societal empathy towards individuals with narcissistic tendencies, in contrast to the understanding and compassion often extended to those experiencing other forms of mental illnesses.

FACTORS THAT CONTRIBUTE TO THE DEVELOPMENT OF NARCISSISTIC PERSONALITY DISORDER (NPD)

Narcissistic Personality Disorder (NPD) does not arise from a singular causative factor. While it is widely acknowledged that genetics likely contribute, there is also a prevailing belief in the significance of early life experiences. Children who have been subjected to abuse, neglect, or trauma, such as those aforementioned, may be at risk. The presence of a parent who exhibits narcissistic tendencies or engages in a consistently critical manner may also give rise to potential risks. Regardless of the underlying factors, these young individuals develop a diminished sense of self and a strong inclination towards seeking validation from external sources.

Numerous individuals with narcissistic tendencies exhibit significantly low levels of self-esteem. These traits contribute to the tendency of individuals to exaggerate their capabilities or accomplishments. They consistently seek recognition and approval from their peers. This constitutes a crucial element in comprehending the individuals exhibiting narcissistic tendencies in your life. Their behavior exhibits an air of hubris and self-centeredness, driven by underlying sentiments of inferiority.

Indicators of Narcissistic Personality Disorder (NPD)

A heightened sense of personal significance

The primary characteristic of narcissism is a pronounced sense of grandeur. Grandiosity extends beyond mere arrogance or conceit, encompassing an inflated sense of superiority. Narcissistic individuals hold the belief that they are unique and that the typical person lacks the ability to comprehend them. Moreover, they reject anything that is mediocre or commonplace. They solely seek to affiliate and forge connections exclusively with individuals, locations, and entities of elevated status.

Narcissistic individuals also harbor an unwavering belief in their superiority over others and exhibit an incessant need for recognition, irrespective of their lack of accomplishments warranting such acclaim. They frequently embellish their accomplishments and level of expertise. In discussions pertaining to their occupations or personal connections, their focus will predominantly lie on the extent of their benevolence, their exceptional qualities, and the fortunate nature of their presence in the lives of others.

They reside in a fictitious realm that fosters their sense of superiority.
Due to the contrast between the reality they face and their grandiose self-perception, narcissists inhabit an illusory realm characterized by deception and self-deception. They invoke self-centered visions of boundless wealth, influence, intellect, attractiveness, and flawless affection that engender a sense of superiority and control.

Facts and perspectives that oppose these notions are dismissed or rationalized, as these illusions shield individuals from experiencing inner void and culpability. Individuals who possess narcissistic tendencies tend to exhibit great defensiveness or even anger when faced with anything that has the potential to disrupt their cherished illusion or facade. Consequently, those in close proximity to the narcissist develop a cautious approach in navigating the intricacies of their denial of objective truth.

A continuous display of reverence and admiration is necessary.

The perception of superiority held by a narcissist resembles a balloon that gradually deflates unless upheld by a constant flow of admiration and recognition. The sporadic expression of approval proves to be inadequate. Due to the narcissists' desire for constant validation, they tend to associate themselves with individuals who are willing to cater to their incessant hunger for admiration.

These are one-sided partnerships. The focus consistently lies on what the admirer has to offer the narcissist, with no reciprocal consideration. The narcissist interprets any interruption or decrease in the admirer's focus and admiration as an act of betrayal.

Feelings of entitlement
Narcissistic individuals desire preferential treatment owing to their perception of being distinct from others. They genuinely believe that they ought to possess whatever they desire. Additionally, they anticipate prompt compliance from others with regard to their every need and desire.

That is their sole value. One's value is diminished if they fail to anticipate and fulfill every expectation placed upon them. If one were to dauntlessly oppose their desires or express a desire for reciprocation, it can be anticipated that acts of violence, indignation, or aloofness may ensue.

They engage in the exploitation of individuals without experiencing any sense of remorse or shame.
Narcissistic individuals do not acquire the ability to empathize with the emotions of others and understand their perspective, thereby failing to effectively place themselves in the position of their victims. They lack empathy. They perceive individuals in their lives as mere objects, existing solely to fulfill their desires. Consequently, they exhibit no hesitation in exploiting others to advance their personal objectives.

Occasionally, this interpersonal exploitation is deliberate, although it is predominantly inadvertent. Narcissists exhibit a disregard for the impact their actions have on others. Despite your efforts to highlight the matter, they will deliberately choose not to comprehend.

Frequently, they engage in the act of disparaging, coercing, harassing, or deriding individuals.

Narcissists experience a sense of threat when encountering individuals who possess qualities or attributes they lack, especially in cases where these individuals exhibit confidence and popularity. Individuals who refrain from exhibiting subservience towards them or expressing any form of dissent equally pose a threat to them. Disdain serves as their defensive mechanism.

In order to mitigate the risk and simultaneously enhance their weakened self-esteem, it is necessary to dismantle those individuals. They may engage in such behavior in a patronizing or disdainful manner, as if to demonstrate their utter disregard for the other individual's significance. In order to reestablish conformity, individuals may employ derogatory remarks, character assassinations, intimidation tactics, and promises of harm.

****

It can prove challenging to discern the presence of a narcissistic individual within the vicinity. They are the individuals who actively engage with the audience, energetically presenting captivating narratives that evoke a sense of importance and accomplishment, thereby cultivating a sense of respect. An individual who conducts themselves in such a manner effectively conveys to all those in their vicinity that they are, in fact, not easily approachable or sympathetic.

Narcissistic individuals frequently display ten out of the following thirteen attributes:

Self-centered - Displays an attitude that suggests the belief that everything revolves around him or her.
Exercising privileges - Establishes and violates regulations
Puts you down
Demands - of whatever he or she desires.
Skeptical - Exhibiting doubts regarding your motives while maintaining politeness towards the person in question.

Paragon of perfection - Exceptionally exacting criteria - unwavering adherence to their own methodology

Snobbish - Thinks he or she is superior to you and others; easily bored

Requesting validation - Seeks continual commendation and recognition.

Lack of enthusiasm - Demonstrating disinterest or a lack of understanding towards your inner thoughts and feelings.

Lack of Remorse - Incapable of offering a heartfelt apology

Excessively focused - Demonstrates an extreme preoccupation with particulars and intricacies.

Dependent - Incapable of relinquishing detrimental behaviors; depends on them for emotional comfort.

Lacks emotional connection - avoids experiencing emotions.

Individuals diagnosed with narcissistic personality disorder often struggle with effectively managing criticism and may display the following behaviors:

become perturbed or incensed when they do not receive specific attention

Experience significant interpersonal challenges and display heightened sensitivity

Respond with intense anger or disgust, and make efforts to disparage the individual in order to assert dominance or superiority.

Encounter challenges in regulating emotions and behavior, significant difficulties in adapting to change and effectively managing stress.

Experience a sense of melancholy and irritability due to their inability to meet perfect standards.

OVERT VS. COVERT NARCISSISM

Covert narcissists exhibit distinctions from overt narcissists solely by virtue of their greater introversion. The explicit manifestation of narcissism can be easily identified due to its characteristic traits of being vocal, boastful, indifferent towards the well-being of others, and perpetually seeking admiration.

Their behavior is easily observable to onlookers, and they have a commanding presence within a room. Overt narcissists demonstrate a greater inclination towards extroversion when it comes to their interactions with others.

The term covert is frequently employed to insinuate that the covert narcissist exhibits cunning characteristics or possesses less pronounced aspirations for prominence compared to an overt (more extroverted) narcissist.

Individuals characterized by narcissistic traits, regardless of whether they exhibit them subtly or prominently, maneuver through life with a pronounced sense of their own significance and indulge in elaborate daydreams of accomplishments and greatness.

To be deemed afflicted with narcissistic personality disorder, individuals exhibiting either overt or covert narcissistic traits must satisfy equal clinical criteria, irrespective of their extraversion or introversion. Both individuals exhibit deficiencies in their capacity to regulate their self-worth.

Numerous individuals have unwittingly become victims of the insidious tactics employed by a covert narcissist, only to realize their plight when they find themselves in a state of emotional turmoil. It could be argued that identifying the extroverted (overt) narcissist is relatively easier compared to discerning the presence of the introverted (covert) narcissist.

ATTRIBUTES OF AN UNDERCOVER NARCISSIST

If you suspect that you are interacting with an individual who exhibits covert narcissistic traits, there are specific overarching attributes and recurrent behavioral patterns that you can observe in your daily interactions.

Having knowledge of these traits can enhance your ability to identify and steer clear of potentially detrimental circumstances, thereby granting you a sense of empowerment.

Importance of Passive Self

The concealed narcissist may exhibit a lower degree of visibility compared to the overt, outgoing narcissist in terms of their inflated self-perception and haughtiness during social interactions.

The covert narcissist craves recognition and adulation, although this may appear inconspicuous to observers. They might engage in the act of giving veiled compliments or intentionally downplay their achievements or skills, with the intention of seeking affirmation from others regarding their capabilities. It remains a verifiable truth that both overt and covert narcissists possess a deficient sense of self.

The overt narcissist seeks adulation and attention, while the covert narcissist employs more subtle tactics to achieve the desired outcomes. The clandestine narcissist will seek consistent validation regarding their aptitudes, competence, and accomplishments by actively seeking individuals who can satiate their insatiable desire for self-significance.

Shaming and Blaming

The act of shaming is employed by individuals with narcissistic tendencies as a means of upholding their sense of superiority in relation to others. The explicit (outgoing) narcissist employs a tactic of gaining advantage that is more conspicuous, characterized by openly belittling, displaying impoliteness, offering criticism, and utilizing sarcasm towards you.

The reserved and concealed nature of the narcissist with introverted tendencies may adopt a more tactful manner when elucidating why responsibility lies with you and not with them. They may even assert themselves as a target of your behavior or engage in psychological mistreatment in order to gain solace and accolades from you. The objective, whether explicit or implicit, is to diminish the other individual's sense of significance.

Creating Confusion
Whilst not inherently characterized by cunning, certain covert narcissists derive satisfaction from inducing ambiguity. Rather than engaging in accusations or humiliation, they prompt individuals to reconsider their perspectives and question their own beliefs.

The covert narcissist employs such tactics in order to assert dominance and maintain authority in the discourse, thereby striving to exert control over the other individual. If they are successful in instilling doubt in your beliefs, it will grant them further chances to exert control and exploit you.

Disregard and Procrastination

Due to the intense extent of their personal need for recognition, covert narcissists will employ every possible measure to ensure that attention remains directed towards them. While an extroverted narcissist may overtly disregard or manipulate others to pursue their goals, the covert narcissist possesses a high level of proficiency in completely disregarding the presence of others.

It comes as little astonishment that individuals with narcissistic tendencies typically gravitate towards affectionate and compassionate individuals. The clandestine narcissist possesses a cognizance of the possibility for manipulation as well. They harbor no reservations when it comes to expressing the notion that you are insignificant.

Instead of outright expressing your insignificance, individuals may decline your invitation for a rendezvous, exhibit delayed responses to your messages or emails, consistently arrive tardily, or abstain from making any concrete commitments whatsoever. Your time and interests receive no regard or acknowledgement, resulting in a diminishment of your importance and relevance.

Giving with a Purpose

By and large, individuals with narcissistic traits tend to exhibit a lack of generosity. They encounter challenges when it comes to directing their endeavors towards endeavors that do not yield personal benefits. A clandestine narcissist may perceive themselves as benevolent, however their acts of generosity are merely a means to attain reciprocal benefits.

They ensure that they establish a form of communication that allows them to receive compliments for their acts of giving. The act of giving often reveals more about the underlying narcissistic tendencies of the giver rather than truly prioritizing the recipients of their generosity.

Neglectful of Emotions

Narcissists demonstrate considerable challenges in establishing and sustaining emotional connections with individuals. The covert narcissist is not an anomaly in this regard. Consequently, despite their outward appearance being more pleasing and less bothersome compared to their extroverted equivalent, they also lack emotional accessibility and receptiveness.

A covert narcissist may not engage in excessive praise towards you. Considering their perpetual preoccupation with seeking superiority in order to maintain their inflated sense of self-worth, it becomes evident why an individual with covert narcissistic tendencies might struggle to acknowledge your value. A narcissist often exhibits a notable lack of regard for your skills or abilities—indeed, there is frequently a complete absence of concern on the part of a narcissist regarding these matters.

In a relationship with a covert narcissist, it is highly probable that you would assume the primary responsibility for the arduous emotional labor, akin to your experience with an overt narcissist.

While the covert behavior may appear to be more emotionally reachable, it generally constitutes a carefully orchestrated act designed to exploit or as a final result, leave the person experiencing feelings of insignificance through disregard, accusation, or disgrace.

Due to the absence of empathy being a foundational trait of narcissistic personality disorder, the covert narcissist will not display a psychologically sound emotional responsiveness towards their spouse.

Please note that individuals who possess covert narcissistic tendencies commonly display behavior characterized by passive aggression. They disregard others while placing emphasis on their own importance. Furthermore, they levell allegations, subject others to humiliation, and exhibit a disregard for the emotions and needs of others.

It can prove challenging to commence anew, amidst the uncharted landscapes and foreign milieu of a different nation. Moving can be an arduous task, and establishing new friendships as an adult in a foreign land can amplify the complexity of the situation. And why is this? As you engage with individuals who possess a more comprehensive comprehension of the nation, you will establish fresh connections. Additionally, they possess the benefit of preexisting established friendships as well as various variables such as upbringing and cultural disparities.

They already possess a superior position and various benefits in comparison to you. It appears as though you are reliving your experience at kindergarten. Hence, it is of utmost significance that you thoroughly evaluate the individuals you permit to enter your life. The transmission of energy can be influential, as individuals may feign agreement in order to maintain inclusion within their social group.

This is the point at which establishing clear delineations becomes crucial. It is possible that they might disclose your personal information to third parties, thereby potentially leveraging this information against you in the future. Additionally, exercise caution when discussing previous traumatic experiences, as certain individuals may not possess the ability to offer the appropriate guidance and assistance that you may necessitate.

A therapist who has undergone comprehensive training is more proficient in offering appropriate counseling, and it is important to note that they are legally bound to maintain strict confidentiality, prohibiting the use of any disclosed information against you. It is imperative to be cautious when confiding in individuals who lack the necessary understanding and means to support you through your trauma, as there is a risk of them spreading confidential information to others. Regrettably, some of these individuals may exploit your vulnerable state for their own gain, thereby exacerbating the harm inflicted upon you rather than providing any meaningful assistance. For individuals of this nature, information holds great strategic value.

Establish boundaries with every individual you encounter.

It may appear perplexing as one experiences relocation to a foreign land devoid of acquaintances, as the primary focus becomes establishing rapid social connections rather than establishing personal boundaries. I can assure you that within a few months, once you have developed a deeper acquaintance with your new acquaintances, you will likely find it desirable to establish certain limits or guidelines with them.

Boundaries can manifest in various ways; for example, it may be necessary to assertively address and denounce any instances of deception directed towards you. By consistently tolerating such behavior, you are effectively conveying to potential exploiters that you lack established criteria and are receptive to any form of mistreatment directed towards you. Indeed, allow your boundaries to be the initial impression they have of you. Assuming responsibility for one's life as a mature individual entails establishing clear boundaries with others.

It is highly advisable to limit the extent of personal information disclosed to others.

As the months elapsed, a strong bond formed between Tayo and me. She assumed the role of an elder sibling figure in my life, frequently extending invitations for me to aid her in various endeavors whenever I was not occupied with my duties. Due to her passion for cooking, I would make a point to rise early on Saturdays in order to lend my assistance. In the event that she was not engaging in culinary activities, she would alternatively be providing assistance with her academic assignments given her status as a post-graduate student.

Occasionally, we would engage in retail therapy, as I was employed at Walmart and had access to the staff discount benefit. On alternate occasions, I would assist her in arranging her hair, and she took great delight in the presence of the younger women from our church, who provided her with pleasant companionship. She extended her assistance and guidance to anyone among us who required aid or counsel, particularly during the height of the COVID-19 outbreak, when widespread confusion prevailed. Particularly in my case, given the absence of any of my relatives residing in Canada.

Initially, she exhibited strong communication skills and displayed a non-judgmental demeanor. After eight months of being together, Tayo inquired about my potential interest in assuming the role of administrative assistant at her spouse's medical practice. I perceived it as a favorable proposition. I had recently commenced my second program at the educational institution when the employment opportunity presented itself, boasting elevated remuneration and marginally greater adaptability compared to my existing occupation. As my rapport with her was flourishing, I harbored no semblance of doubt regarding the merit of collaborating with them.

A week after the interview was scheduled, the interview was conducted at their residence. While I initially perceived this new offer as a viable progression in my career, my intuition imparted a contrasting perspective. As a result, I refrained from tendering a complete resignation from Walmart.

While being interviewed, Tayo inquired about my ability to uphold boundaries and exhibit professionalism, taking into account my affiliation as a church member. I provided her with reassurance that I would fulfill the task, as I perceived no potential complications. I was extended an employment opportunity and commenced my duties in the month of October.

Pastor Ola's practice consisted of two locations, one situated in Durham and the other in Toronto. At first, I was exclusively employed for work at the Toronto office; however, it was subsequently determined that I should operate from both locations. The intended arrangement was for me to allocate three days to work in Toronto and two days at the Durham office. Although I possess significant expertise in administration, I would also contribute to the organization as a marketing communications professional, thereby enhancing the business's visibility and customer service.

Another notable aspect of my new employment was its enhanced flexibility in terms of working hours; it deviated from the conventional nine-to-five schedule. My schedule was organized in accordance with the designated appointment times of the clients. This afforded me additional time to concentrate on my academic pursuits, socializing with acquaintances, or collaborating with Tayo and Deola in culinary endeavors, or any other such activity undertaken during that particular week.

Upon commencing my employment at Pastor Ola's practice, I had been actively participating in the church for nearly ten months, thereby acquainting myself with both him and his spouse. Both individuals exhibited the mannerisms of treating and perceiving me as their younger sibling, and I had the opportunity to formally acquaint them with my mother, brother, and his spouse. I reached a point of sufficient comfort in our relationship where I felt inclined to approach Tayo with a request to designate her as my emergency contact, a proposal which she graciously agreed to.

She possessed a deep understanding and confidence in my abilities, which led her to suggest that I collaborate with her spouse. However, I soon realized my assumption was mistaken. I never harbored the suspicion that she may have had an ulterior motive for endorsing me. It is my presumption that our purpose for being present is to ascertain the truth. One factor to consider is that she undoubtedly did not anticipate my reaction to her unjustifiable demand.

Tayo appeared to be actively engaged in the affairs of the church, placing less emphasis on administrative responsibilities. Additionally, it was evident that nearly everyone in Canada engaged in two forms of employment, namely their primary occupation and an additional source of income commonly referred to as a side hustle. Tayo's formidable presence was consistently apparent in the office, as her imposing demeanor and unwavering insistence on having tasks executed in accordance with her preferences was undeniable. Pastor Ola presented a contrasting perspective in that regard. Tayo made minimal contributions to the office, yet consistently appropriated credit for his accomplishments in the business.

In November, Tayo and I had established a favorable rapport in our friendship. Both of us had gained some additional understanding of one another, and she appeared sufficiently at ease to request that I pass along particular information to her spouse. As an illustration, in circumstances where she disapproved of the sermon delivered by her husband in the church, or desired that I adhere to specific methods in the workplace, she would propose that I communicate these sentiments to him, attributing them to my own perception to ensure her spouse remained unaware of her involvement. I consistently engaged in this practice, and subsequently discovered that fellow members of the church were also partaking in such acts of assistance on her behalf.

Upon our initial encounter, I confidently assert that Tayo proved to be the most amiable individual I had ever encountered in my entire existence. I would quickly discover, however, that her pleasant demeanor came with a substantial price. Due to her cordiality towards me, I had not previously regarded her assertive nature as being controlling. Initially, it seems that my perception of her was limited to her affable demeanor. Each time she exhibited behavior that was peculiar or deviated from her usual conduct, I would provide justifications on her behalf.

An additional peculiar observation I made was that on numerous occasions, she would consistently misconstrue or misinterpret any remarks I would make towards her. One instance that exemplifies this occurred when she attempted to arrange a romantic relationship for me with a family acquaintance who also happened to be previously married. While attempting to communicate to her that I was not prepared for a romantic commitment, and that I was unable to envision a future with him, particularly due to the significant age gap of over twenty years, she subsequently conveyed to her spouse that I expressed a strong dislike towards Mr. Divorcee and found him to be quite bothersome. Discuss the film 'Lost in Translation'.

Despite consistently extending her offer to provide guidance to the new individual, she ultimately failed to follow through on this commitment. What she engaged in was the act of extending her personal possessions to me, with the intention of fostering a recurring dependency on her for further assistance. On one occasion, whenever I inquired about the sources for procuring Nigerian food items, she consistently refrained from providing a definitive response, instead suggesting that I either obtain or purchase the required items directly from her.

Initially, my perception of the individual was favorable, as they seemed amiable. However, I failed to discern their ulterior motive, which ultimately proved to be a conventional strategy of exerting control and manipulation. I inquired of Pastor Ola regarding the availability of Nigerian food items, only to discover a store conveniently located a mere five minutes from the office. Additionally, it was revealed that the proprietor of said store was previously affiliated with our church community.

After the passage of nine months, our relationship had grown exceptionally strong, so much so that in early December, she graciously granted me admission into the esteemed women's church WhatsApp group. This facilitated my ease in confiding in her regarding certain past traumas I have experienced. She expressed her support and made a commitment to assist me in overcoming them. But instead of keeping to her promise, she started using my vulnerability against me. The subsequent chapters will reveal the unfolding of events.

Eft Tapping

EFT, alternatively known as Emotional Freedom Technique, is an uncomplicated method of acupressure that provides the means to swiftly alleviate the emotional distress caused by narcissistic abuse.

This particular approach to healing is somewhat more contentious compared to the other methods mentioned, primarily due to the fact that, while it does garner some level of endorsement from the field of clinical psychology, there remains an ongoing discussion regarding its efficacy beyond mere placebo response. However, numerous alternative healing methodologies, such as acupressure and energy medicine, have a longstanding history and are considered venerable traditions. It is occasionally employed for the alleviation of physical discomfort, yet its more common application lies in mitigating emotional anguish, such as anxiety and post-traumatic stress disorder (PTSD). I have personally found it to be efficacious in addressing the anxiety that has manifested as a consequence of my father's narcissistic maltreatment.

If one exhibits certain symptoms, they may identify the occurrence of an attack or flashback associated with narcissistic abuse.

• Cold sensations or sudden warmth

• Accelerated or palpitations of the cardiac rhythm

• Overwhelmed by an intense sense of dread, as if an imminent catastrophe is looming.

• Cardiac discomfort • Thoracic distress

• Pain in the chest cavity • Angina pectoris

• Apprehension towards engaging in actions that may result in embarrassment or a loss of control

- Symptoms of nausea, lightheadedness, and dizziness are present.
- Sensation of numbness or tingling in the hands
- Difficulties with respiration

These attacks are marked by their capricious nature, rendering anticipation and detection difficult, if not impossible. EFT tapping can be employed at any location and on any occasion to effectively halt an attack.

Allow me to provide you with a comprehensive guide on how to administer self-treatment.

Employ your middle and index fingers to delicately tap on each designated spot, consecutively and for a duration of three seconds, thus prompting the revitalization of your energy points.

Top of your head

Brow region: the portion of the eyebrow proximal to the nasal area.

The lateral aspect of the eye, located at the outermost corner of the orbit.

Beneath each eye, situated on the upper region of the cheekbone.

Under the nose

Under the lips

Under the clavicle

Located at a distance of four inches beneath the axillary region on the lateral aspect of your body

Utilize a single hand to make contact with either one or both aspects of the physique and countenance. Commence by gently pressing on the metacarpal region adjacent to the little finger, directing your attention towards the issue at hand. You will start to experience feelings of anxiety and apprehension. Proceed by gently tapping on the designated spots while recalling your apprehensive thoughts or past encounters.

Healing a memory requires the elimination of the emotions evoked when one recollects that particular memory. You will possess the capacity to recall your prior experiences without eliciting any immediate response. In the event that feelings of anxiety arise, accompanied by an accelerated heart rate or the sensation of dryness in the oral cavity during the recollection process, it signifies that the aforementioned memory remains unhealed and in a vulnerable state. Utilize the technique of EFT tapping in conjunction with recollection of the assault until its emotional intensity diminishes. Tell yourself, "It happened. The ordeal has concluded, I have emerged unharmed, and I am in a satisfactory state."

Yoga

Yoga provides a pathway for individuals to facilitate the healing process from traumatic experiences by effectively regulating their hormonal balance. Throughout the period of mistreatment, your amygdala exhibited heightened activity and there was a continual release of cortisol in your system. Your physical form was in a perpetual state of engagement, tirelessly endeavoring to persevere. Yoga enables the cessation of the fight-or-flight response, thus affording the body an opportunity to undergo healing.

This is the manner in which I commence my pre-sleep regimen. I engage in yoga practice, engage in meditation, and subsequently retire to bed. This situation has persisted ever since I implemented the decision to disengage from all communication with my father. It has proven to be a valuable asset in navigating numerous challenges. I am cognizant of the fact that this is the singular aspect upon which I can rely without fail on a daily basis.

Presented below are a selection of yoga postures that can be employed to facilitate the release of trauma and foster the ongoing process of healing:

Bound Angle Pose

To execute the exercise, assume a seated position on a yoga mat or a towel while extending your legs in front of you. Draw your feet inward, towards your pelvis, until the soles of your feet make contact. Permit your knees to descend to their maximum extent. Please maintain a firm grip on this object for a brief duration, then proceed to let go.

Pond Pose

Assume a supine position on a yoga mat. Please flex your knees and draw your heels towards your hips to the fullest extent possible, ensuring that your feet remain approximately one and a half feet apart. Elevate your arms upwards and encircle them around your head, allowing all the muscles throughout your body to unwind. Please maintain the position momentarily before gradually lowering your feet.

Upward-Facing Dog

Assume a prone position by lying flat on your abdomen, ensuring that your hands are resting flat beneath your shoulders. Elevate your body by extending your arms, thereby raising your chest, abdomen, upper thighs, knees, and shins from the surface. The tops of your feet should be flat on the floor. Ensure that your shoulders remain relaxed and avoid the upward pulling of the muscles. Please retain momentarily and then release.

Lion Pose

Assume a kneeling posture with your buttocks resting upon your legs. Please position your hands on the ground, directly before your knees. Please gently extend your hands forward to achieve a position in which you are leaning slightly over your knees, maintaining a straight back and ensuring that your neck aligns with your spine. Direct your gaze forward, part your lips, and allow your tongue to dangle gracefully akin to the majestic stance of a lion. Please maintain pressure for a brief period and then release.

Pyramid Pose

Assume a stance with the positioning of one foot slightly advanced in front of the other. The rear foot should be slightly inclined outward. Interlock your hands behind your back and gradually assume a forward-leaning position. Lower your hands towards the ground, placing them on either side of your front feet. It is imperative that you orient your head in a downward direction. Please pause momentarily and gradually ascend back to the original position. Perform the same action on the opposite flank.

Arm Swings

Position yourself with your feet at a hip-width distance, and initiate a rotational movement of your torso, alternating between the left and right sides. Permit your arms to relax and drape loosely around your torso. Once you have achieved a state of relaxation, gradually decrease the velocity of arm movement until it comes to a complete cessation.

Headstand

This task is of an advanced nature. Therefore, it is advisable not to proceed with it if you lack comfort or familiarity. Please kneel down and gently touch the top of your head to the ground. Embrace your head with your arms. Lift a single foot from the ground, bringing the knee up and towards your chest. Gently and gradually remove the remaining foot from the surface, then cautiously elevate your legs until they are fully extended in a vertical position. Maintain the position for as long as it is feasible for you, while gradually descending your legs.

Zumba

Engaging in physical activity is consistently beneficial for alleviating stress, including that which is linked to post-traumatic stress disorder (PTSD). Nevertheless, certain types of exercise possess a slightly greater potential for stress reduction than others. Zumba is an exercise fitness program that bears resemblance to Jazzercise and originated in the 1990s through the efforts of Alberto "Beto" Pérez, a renowned Colombian dancer and choreographer. It employs salsa, reggaeton, merengue, and cumbia as its core rhythmic elements.

Zumba can offer contrasting benefits for individuals who have experienced narcissistic abuse, when compared to the benefits provided by yoga. Instead of equilibrium and tranquility, it will provide you with a channel for repressed energy and a surge of force. Both activities facilitate the development of coordination, posture, and body control. It should be noted that neither of them can be deemed as right or wrong. Alternatively, they are distinct approaches to establishing a connection with one's body and inner self.

Moreover, besides the evident cardiovascular advantages and the potential for weight reduction and calorie burn, Zumba offers significant emotional benefits. Primarily, engaging in any form of physical activity leads to the secretion of endorphins, which are innate mood-enhancers. This effect is subsequently amalgamated with the vibrant rhythm of the music, thereby augmenting the release of additional endorphins and further elevating one's mood. Furthermore, Zumba has the potential to enhance one's self-assurance. Participating in the dance routines incorporated into the exercise regimen will entail focusing on improving your body alignment and enhancing your motor skills, potentially prompting you to venture beyond your accustomed boundaries. The aforementioned reduction in weight and calories will also enhance your appearance, thereby bolstering your self-perception and instilling greater self-assurance within you.

An additional advantage offered by Zumba is the opportunity to become a part of a community. If you opt to enroll in a program instead of relying solely on online videos (which is also a viable option), you will have the opportunity to immerse yourself in a community of individuals who are all actively pursuing a shared objective: engagement in this distinctive form of exercise. You will have the opportunity to remain in the vicinity, engage in conversation with unfamiliar individuals, and establish a community that you may choose to include in your inner circle once you feel comfortable enough to share your story with them. In a similar vein as any community, there is an inherent sense of comfort in the knowledge that there exists a designated place and supportive individuals to turn to in times of need.

There are ten diverse levels of classes catering to varying age groups and exertion levels, hence ostensibly ensuring accessibility for all individuals to partake. You have the option to enroll in an authorized Zumba Fitness, LLC course taught by a certified instructor, or alternatively, you can conduct a search for "Zumba" on the online platform YouTube where you will discover an abundance of complementary video tutorials enabling you to alleviate stress through the joy of dance.

Narcissist In A Relationship

A considerable number of individuals are unaware of the potential hazards associated with having a self-centered partner. The encounter is far from pleasant, as individuals displaying egotistical tendencies tend to demonstrate selfishness, harm, manipulation, and inflict various forms of emotional exploitation and suffering upon their victims.

Individuals with an inherent self-centered nature suffer from Narcissistic Personality Disorder due to their lack of empathy and genuine emotional understanding. Similarly, it can be incredibly perplexing to navigate relationships with self-centered partners due to their tendency to exhibit kindness towards you one day and contempt the next. They typically encounter difficulty in determining whether to value or loathe you. As a result of this, numerous individuals associated with individuals exhibiting egomaniacal tendencies attempt to understand their incessant fluctuation between affection and detachment.

In this section, we will undertake a more comprehensive examination of the behavior of the egotist when experiencing love, delving from a higher-level perspective to a more detailed analysis. This will aid you in determining whether your partner exhibits egotistical traits, and if you genuinely desire to extricate yourself from this detrimental relationship.

The Amorous Cycle of Narcissistic Individuals

Frequently, it is often beyond the realm of comprehension that one is dealing with an individual driven by excessive self-importance and egotism. In light of this, achieving a complete separation poses challenges. Certain individuals would have devoted a considerable duration of time in the company of the egomaniac and ought to consider marrying and procreating. Furthermore, certain individuals become ensnared in toxic relationships, developing a sense of reliance despite enduring significant harm from their association with a narcissist.

To be fully candid, due to the machinations of an egotistical person, certain individuals may come to acknowledge their inadequacy for superior opportunities and believe they are undeserving of the best. These individuals have continuously experienced mistreatment and have been devalued, leading them to adopt the belief of their inherent worthlessness over time.

What is the nature of a narcissist's love?

The egomaniac displays distinctive behavior in regards to ordinary individuals when experiencing affection.

We will be examining their demonstration of affection in order to highlight it.

Throwing Bait

When evaluating an individual with excessive self-importance from the outset, it is often observed that they excel in the art of deception. Egotistical individuals often initiate relationships with acts of goodwill and a display of warmth. They will bestow upon you affection and accolades. They will present themselves with great kindness towards you and will exert all efforts to ensure your complete admiration and submission.

In the beginning stages of a relationship with an individual exhibiting egomaniacal tendencies, you may have harbored utmost conviction that you had finally found the quintessential partner. It appears excessively profound to fathom, and one wishes for its continuity. You may have been bestowed with praise, recognition, presents, endorsement, outings, and dinners that convinced you that you are in the presence of your true love and soulmate. This initial phase is referred to as the stage of courtship. At this juncture, individuals with egotistical tendencies will make earnest efforts to show that they possess genuine affection for you. Upon accepting this, they express their satisfaction in ensnaring you and replacing the previous demonstration of affection with a form of abuse, thereby dehumanizing and debasing you. In the course of carrying out these actions, they display a lack of awareness regarding their errors and avoid assuming responsibility for their conduct. Taking everything into account, they will lay blame upon you for any occurrences in view of the fact that you do not adhere to their misguided notion of who you should be or your true identity. As time passes, one finds themselves reminiscing about the moments of joy while grappling with the challenges of everyday life.

Notwithstanding, individuals with excessive self-importance may occasionally exhibit affection towards you through the bestowal of journeys or presents; however, such displays ultimately fail to endure. Prior to immersing yourself in the external facade of rejuvenated affection, you find yourself confronted once again with the arduous struggle and another cycle of degradation. The feelings of futility gradually emerge, rendering you once again immobile.

Their rationale for undertaking this action stems directly from their trust in conditional associations and their fondness for unpredictable happiness. Their primary objective commonly revolves around attaining personal contentment and gratification, as well as the necessity to enhance their self-assurance. Individuals with egotistical tendencies acknowledge that social interactions can be seen as strategic endeavors, where achieving victory becomes the primary objective. Their primary concern lies in achieving dominance in the match, and that is their sole focus. However, on every occasion in which they have had the opportunity to ensnare you, they reveal their true disposition through their manipulative behavior.

They Are Manipulative

Numerous individuals with narcissistic tendencies have the ability to convince others to enter into a romantic relationship with them due to their charismatic and captivating personality. They also possess the ability to survive, comprehend, and articulate emotions due to their possession of the skill to perceive individuals on a more profound level. In addition, they possess a manipulative nature that allows them to gain the admiration and affection of others. They exhibit manipulative tendencies and employ various tactics to ensure that you experience a sense of unease, utilizing defamation as a means to instill feelings of inferiority within you.

They engage in this behavior out of consideration for your sensitivity and vulnerability. They rely on their tendency to proudly extol their merits and actively seek gratification. They also exhibit amiability and have the ability to leave a remarkable first impression upon initial interaction. Several individuals with narcissistic tendencies exhibit remarkable qualities in their ability to convey affection, romance, sweet expressions, and unwavering commitments, thus appearing to be exceptional lovers. Similarly, they employ deceit in order to convince their confederate of their deep self-love, conveying it through tangible possessions.

Once they are prepared to enlist an accomplice, individuals with extreme self-centeredness tend to experience a waning of interest in intimacy, often encountering difficulties in sustaining a relationship over an extended period. Frequently, they prioritize power over intimacy and have a strong aversion towards weakness, perceiving it as a flaw. They derive pleasure from exerting control over others, as they deem themselves superior to following directives. In this way, they prefer to maintain a distance. Consequently, the optimal approach to resolving their concerns is to engage in collaborations with varying counterparts.

The prolonged ramifications of engaging in a relationship with a narcissist can lead to a dramatic culmination. The severance will occur suddenly, and the former acquaintance is overwhelmed and perplexed by the unexpected termination of the relationship. They are experiencing feelings of disillusionment, exploitation, abandonment, suppression, and perplexity. Nevertheless, in the event that they choose to continue their relationship, they would inevitably come to realize or discover the inherent self-centeredness of their partner.

Occasionally, an individual exhibiting egotistic tendencies may employ a pragmatic approach, thereby directing their focus solely towards their personal objectives. Nevertheless, he may harbor positive sentiments towards a companion or individuals who share a common interest. In the context of matrimony, he falls short in providing the requisite motivation necessary for sustaining a healthy relationship, as he is unable to maintain the facade. On every occasion when this happens, he endeavors to counteract intimacy by exhibiting anger, aloofness, and criticism through the exploration of diverse strategies.

It becomes difficult to confront him due to this, as doing so could potentially give rise to complications. Although egotists may occasionally meet the expectations of their partners at their own discretion, they typically devalue their partners and actively seek opportunities to elevate their already inflated ego elsewhere. Notwithstanding such, generally speaking, individuals with egotistical tendencies tend to maintain their involvement in a relationship and rarely sever ties with a partner as long as they continue to provide value.

The Impact Of Narcissistic Abuse On Affected Individuals

The consequences of narcissistic abuse encompass a spectrum that spans from mild to severe, although it is noteworthy that the majority of individuals experience severe repercussions. Individuals with narcissistic tendencies commonly experience the repercussions of this disorder and are highly prone to grappling with an array of mental conditions, such as depression, anxiety, and diminished self-worth. Individuals who fall prey to narcissistic behavior may also experience the onset of significant mental health conditions, including but not limited to social anxiety or post-traumatic stress disorder. In order to enhance your understanding of the potential consequences that you may encounter, this chapter will be dedicated to educating you about the potential effects and psychological conditions that may emerge as a result of narcissistic abuse.

The Predominant Impact Exerted by Narcissists on Their Targets

I would like to discuss the initial consequence of narcissistic abuse, which pertains to the development of anxiety disorders. An anxiety disorder is a pathological condition characterized by the manifestation of severe symptoms of anxiety or panic in individuals. Put simply, an anxiety disorder manifests when an individual undergoes intense feelings of anxiety or panic, rendering them incapable of effectively coping with their symptoms. Generalized anxiety disorder (GAD) is the preeminent anxiety disorder stemming from the trauma of narcissistic abuse. As a result of the inherent characteristics of narcissistic abuse, such as erratic emotional outbursts, the need to be overly cautious in one's actions, and the manipulation technique known as gaslighting, a considerable number of individuals who have experienced narcissistic abuse tend to experience heightened levels of anxiety as they progress through life. This spectrum encompasses Generalized Anxiety Disorder (GAD) as well as more profound forms of disorders, including Post-Traumatic Stress Disorder (PTSD).

Anxiety disorder characterized by excessive and persistent worry
Generalized anxiety refers to an inherent inclination to exhibit an excessive level of panic, apprehension, or distress in response to a wide range of events or circumstances. Typically, individuals commonly experience pronounced challenges in regulating their feelings of anxiety, accompanied by additional manifestations such as chronic

weariness, restlessness, impaired focus, sleep disruptions, heightened irritability, and muscular tension. Anxiety can be described as a cognitive process centered around the ambiguity surrounding future occurrences. It is, in fact, not an emotion per se, but rather a catalyst for experiencing feelings of anxiety. The primary and most conspicuous manifestation of generalized anxiety disorder is the emergence of intrusive thoughts centered around potential scenarios or hypotheticals. These contemplations of hypothetical scenarios are intertwined with anxiety, and frequently seem beyond one's ability to manage. Moreover, the process of concern is frequently linked to physiological manifestations that are closely tied to the instinctive fight or flight reaction. Frequently, individuals tend to perceive the future with a pessimistic outlook, giving rise to thoughts that are subsequently accompanied by feelings of anxiety.

Individuals diagnosed with Generalized Anxiety Disorder (GAD) frequently experience a consistent state of apprehension and unease, manifesting as pervasive worry and anxiety rather than being confined to particular stress-inducing circumstances. The concerns they have experienced have persisted, been of great intensity, and significantly disrupted their daily activities. Their concerns typically encompass various facets rather than being limited to a single factor. It might encompass various facets such as employment, well-being, financial matters, familial affairs, or simply routine aspects of daily existence. Inconsequential activities such as domestic obligations or tardiness to a scheduled engagement can precipitate severe agitation, ultimately culminating in a sense of impending catastrophe.

The diagnosis of Generalized Anxiety Disorder (GAD) is typically established when individuals exhibit several symptoms persistently for a duration of at least six months:

You are experiencing a high level of anxiety regarding multiple activities or events.

You find it challenging to cease your concerns.

You are experiencing considerable difficulty in performing your daily activities such as studying, working, and socializing due to the profound influence of your anxiety.

You consistently experience a sense of unease or agitation.

You are always/easily tired.

You struggle with concentration.

You are easily irritable.

You are experiencing muscular tension, particularly in areas such as your neck or jaw that may be causing discomfort.

You are experiencing challenges with sleep (such as experiencing difficulty in maintaining or initiating sleep).

Individuals who lack prior exposure to narcissistic abuse may also be vulnerable to developing Generalized Anxiety Disorder (GAD). This phenomenon is more commonly observed in females as opposed to males and has the potential to manifest at any point throughout an individual's lifespan. This phenomenon is prevalent across all age demographics, encompassing even the very young and the elderly. Nevertheless, the prevalent period for diagnosis typically occurs during an individual's approximate age of 30. Nevertheless, youngsters with a parent or close relative afflicted with narcissism or a familial disorder face an elevated susceptibility to early onset generalized anxiety disorder. They commonly demonstrate tendencies such as:

Having a lack of self-assurance
Being over-conforming
Persistently striving for validation and reassurance from one's peers.
Being a perfectionist
Requiring the redoing of tasks to achieve optimal results.
Utilizing the expression "Affirmative, however, what if?"

In addition to narcissistic abuse, a multitude of factors can contribute to the development of Generalized Anxiety Disorder (GAD). To begin with, primary emphasis is placed on biological factors. GAD has been correlated with specific alterations in brain functioning. Furthermore, the examination of family history is also taken into account. Individuals with Generalized Anxiety Disorder (GAD) frequently exhibit a familial background marked by a prevalence of mental health conditions. Stressful life events can be a contributing factor to the heightened vulnerability of an individual to develop Generalized Anxiety Disorder (GAD). For instance, instances such as the dissolution of a relationship, relocation, or experiences of physical or emotional mistreatment serve as illustrations of events that can contribute to the development of Generalized Anxiety Disorder (GAD). In conclusion, it is worth noting that individuals may face an increased susceptibility due to underlying psychological influences. Individuals who possess characteristics such as sensitivity, anxious disposition, or low frustration tolerance are more susceptible to developing Generalized Anxiety Disorder (GAD).

Panic Disorder

Panic disorders, more commonly referred to as panic attacks, are characterized by the recurring and incapacitating nature of these episodes. In instances where individuals experience acute anxiety, particular circumstances, or even in the absence of external stimuli, they may be susceptible to entering a state of uncontrollable panic, rendering them unable to regain composure or alleviate distress. Individuals who have experienced abuse are at a heightened risk of developing this disorder, as the occurrence of triggering events can lead to the manifestation of severe anxiety symptoms. Typically, panic disorders are characterized by:

Surprising and recurrent episodes of panic.

Continuously experiencing distress for an extended period of time (one month) following a panic attack will result in the occurrence of another episode.

Concerning oneself with the potential ramifications subsequent to experiencing a panic attack. Many individuals may hold the belief that a panic attack is indicative of an undisclosed medical condition. For instance, individuals may undergo multiple medical examinations in response to such concerns, yet despite negative results, they continue to harbor apprehension regarding their physical well-being.

Exhibiting pronounced behavioral shifts associated with episodes of panic attacks. For instance, refraining from physical activity due to the potential elevation of your heart rate.

Typically, amidst a panic attack, one experiences an overpowering sensation of the aforementioned physiological manifestations. The climax of a panic attack typically occurs after approximately 10 minutes, with a duration of up to 30 minutes, followed by a state of exhaustion. They can take place frequently within a day or infrequently over a span of a year. These occurrences can occur during a person's slumber, subsequently inducing them to awaken amid the episode. A considerable number of individuals have, in fact, encountered a panic attack at least once throughout their lifetimes. A panic attack has been known to occur in up to 40% of the global populace during the course of their lifetimes. This does not imply the presence of a panic disorder. Listed below are the typical indicators and manifestations associated with a panic attack: "

A sensation of immense dread or anxiety.
Experiencing the perception of asphyxiation, demise, or a state of irrationality.
Heart rate increases
Experiencing respiratory distress (such as rapid or shallow breathing)"
Experiencing sensations of constriction in the throat or impaired respiratory function.
Perspiring excessively
Episodes of lightheadedness, dizziness, or fainting

In certain instances, individuals undergoing a panic attack may also encounter states of dissociation or derealization. These states manifest as a perceptual experience wherein one perceives the world and their surroundings as lacking in authenticity or veracity. This symptom is correlated with the profound physiological alterations occurring in the body during the course of this anxiety episode.

Panic disorders exhibit lower prevalence rates compared to other disorders such as general anxiety disorder (GAD) or social anxiety. Surprisingly, a significant portion—specifically, 5%—of the population has been a victim of panic disorder at some point in their lives. Based on statistical data, the prevalence of panic disorders tends to be higher among women than men. Panic disorders generally manifest during early to mid-20s or the midpoint of one's life. Indeed, it holds factual veracity that panic disorders have the potential to manifest at any stage of life;

notwithstanding, instances of occurrence in children or elderly individuals are exceedingly infrequent.

What is the precise etiology of panic disorder? Although a definitive cause cannot be identified, it is typically observed that several factors are commonly implicated. This encompasses individuals who have a familial background of anxiety disorders or depressive illnesses. There is even evidence to suggest that genetics exerts a significant influence in this regard. Panic disorders can also be linked to physiological factors such as asthma, irritable bowel syndrome (IBS), and hyperthyroidism. Adverse life events significantly contribute to the development of panic disorders. Panic disorders have been found to be associated with highly distressing life events such as sexual abuse or the loss of a loved one. Furthermore, individuals who are currently experiencing severe and prolonged stress are highly susceptible to the development of panic disorders.

Ensuring Self-Preservation Against A Manipulative Relative Engaging In Gaslighting

Should you come to the realization that, despite your sincere efforts, you consistently face a lack of acknowledgement or acceptance within your familial environment, it is plausible that an individual (such as your parents, siblings, or other relatives) is engaging in the practice of gaslighting. This occurrence is quite common within families that apply disparate criteria for dispensing rewards and punishments. In such environments, there is a tendency to accord preferential treatment to a specific family member, often referred to as the 'golden child,' wherein even if they are at fault, they receive relatively lenient disciplinary measures. Alternatively, the scapegoat child consistently receives unfavorable treatment, while their accomplishments are seldom recognized. Conversely, their deficiencies are frequently exaggerated to create a sense of greater displacement. If there arises a conflict between the scapegoat child and the golden child, it is often the former who assumes responsibility for all the misfortunes that occurred. This may lead the child who is being scapegoated to contemplate, "In what manner is this situation solely attributable to me?" Am I overlooking any crucial details, is there a clandestine plot underway, or am I experiencing a lapse in logical reasoning?"

An often observed occurrence in cases of gaslighting among family members is the emergence of the drama triangle. This phenomenon occurs when there is an individual who assumes the role of a victim, another person who assumes the role of a persecutor, and yet another person who assumes the role of a rescuer. The gaslighter, acting as the persecutor, has the ability to subject the victim to oppression by means of bullying and making threats. A neutral third party is required to intervene and assist in rescuing the victim when they become caught in the midst of the persecutor's aggression. As an illustration, when an individual assumes the role of the family's designated scapegoat and engages in a dispute with the favored child, it necessitates the intervention of an impartial party to facilitate a just resolution of the conflict.

Regrettably, it is still possible to experience gaslighting from the rescuer, even if it is unintentional. For instance, in situations where an individual intervenes to address a disagreement and appease both sides, they may assert, "That is incorrect." You are ascribing interpretations to it. It would be advisable to endeavor to put this matter to rest and proceed forward. By doing so, they may have resolved the conflict but disregarded the legitimacy of your emotions. You assert that you are not attributing any significance to the actions of the other individual, yet whenever you interact with them, they consistently dismiss your observations as figments of your imagination. This could potentially lead to one questioning whether the issue resides with oneself.

Additionally, it is not advisable to navigate through one's existence while constantly relying on others to consistently rescue and provide a sense of fulfilment or lack thereof, depending on the circumstances. It is imperative that you take proactive measures to safeguard yourself against the manipulative tactics employed by a family member engaging in gaslighting.

One can effectively shield oneself against gaslighting tactics employed by a family member by employing discretion in choosing one's battles. The dynamics of sibling relationships and parent-child relationships differ significantly from those of friendships or spousal relationships. This can create challenges in disengaging from the manipulative family member. However, it is within your discretion to either address these issues or disregard them, especially considering the fact that it may be difficult to immediately alter your living situation with them. By implementing a notable decrease in interpersonal interactions with them, the likelihood of encountering disputes diminishes.

Do not allow any doubts to enter your mind in regard to yourself and your memories, regardless of any contradictory claims made by others. In the event that you encounter a situation where a parent, whether aware of it or not, engages in the practice of gaslighting, it is advisable to politely remove yourself from their company when they attempt to employ such tactics. Avoid engaging in discussions or conversations that have the potential to elicit disagreement or discord.

Ensuring self-preservation in response to gaslighting from a family member does not necessitate harboring animosity towards them. Maintain a profound reverence towards each individual within your family unit, while also asserting and upholding your own dignity. Do not afford others the opportunity to undermine your self-esteem.

Safeguarding Against Emotional Manipulation by a Partner Exhibiting Gaslighting Behavior

Arguably, the most arduous aspect of safeguarding oneself from a gaslighting partner involves the identification and acknowledgement of such abusive behavior. For many individuals, maintaining objectivity and rationality while dealing with individuals who hold a strong emotional significance can pose significant challenges. The emotion of affection has the potential to obscure their perception of various moral transgressions. To put it differently, individuals who are married to abusive individuals may endure extended periods of time in abusive relationships due to their reluctance to acknowledge the existence of such behavior. Ideas such as, "It is implausible! He possesses too much charisma to harbor any intention of causing harm," "She has remained steadfastly supportive during both the favorable and challenging times." The notion that she would have any intention to cause harm to me, even if I entertain the thought, will perpetuate the suffering endured by victims.

The initial measure that should be undertaken in safeguarding oneself against gaslighting entails adopting a pragmatic and impartial perspective of the circumstances. Psychologically detach yourself from the situation and closely observe the behavior of your spouse. Do you observe a recurring trend of adverse conduct? If your answer is affirmative, it is imperative that you promptly proceed with necessary measures.

It is imperative that one possesses the capacity to disengage from the relationship, even in absence of personal inclination. Do not allow anyone to persuade you into thinking that you are entirely dependent on them or that they possess the ability to prolong a relationship beyond your own desires. If the gaslighter poses a threat to your personal safety, it is imperative that you do not underestimate the gravity of the situation. Report the threat immediately. Certainly, individuals who engage in gaslighting behavior may possess inherent goodness but have experienced emotional dissonance that necessitates healing. However, as you are not a qualified therapist, it is also not within your professional purview to initiate the diagnosis of mental health disorders. In order for an effective self-improvement process to take place, it is imperative that you prioritize addressing your own personal growth. A highly recommended approach to achieving this is to establish significant physical and emotional separation between yourself and the individual who engages in gaslighting behavior. Prioritize establishing your foundation before extending assistance, regardless of whether individuals exhibit narcissistic tendencies or not.

After severing ties with an individual who employs gaslighting tactics, it is imperative to refrain from entertaining any future interactions. It is highly probable that they may exert efforts to reestablish communication, however, it is crucial not to provide them with the opportunity to do so. Chapter 7 will explore a specific tactic employed by gaslighters and emotional abusers to draw their victims back into abusive relationships. For the present moment, let it be understood that upon parting ways with an individual who exhibits gaslighting behavior, it is advisable to firmly shut the entrance to your emotions and permanently renounce any association with them. It is imperative not to cultivate companionship with such individuals. Do not be deceived by the notion that despite our separation, we can maintain a friendly relationship.

In light of your interpersonal dynamics, it would be highly advisable to establish a stronger rapport with individuals whom you deem reliable. However, approach this action with the aim of soliciting assistance rather than attempting to identify someone else to rely upon. Alternative phrasing in a formal tone: "While considering viewpoints from external sources is acceptable, your personal beliefs hold merit." In the event that you opt to safeguard yourself from the manipulative tactics of a gaslighter, it is imperative to possess the unwavering belief in your capacity to navigate and overcome any subsequent trials that may arise in your life.

Ultimately, you need not harbor any animosity towards them. Alternatively, regard your time spent with them as an educational phase. Utilize the insights derived from the relationship to foster personal growth and self-improvement. Abandon the desire to seek retribution and harbor animosity towards them. Engaging in such an action implies that they retain dominion over your mental faculties.

Categories of Co-dependency: Passive, Active, and Variations

Passive and Active Tenses
First and foremost, a co-dependent can be categorized into two distinct groups that involve emotional manipulation. They are, indeed,
Self-centered
Individuals struggling with substance dependency
Altruism
The coexistence of these three stages of co-dependency collectively elucidates the influence of the cofactor of co-dependency, signifying that individuals consistently seek out partners who do not reciprocate mutual support. The respondent exhibits either a passive or active attitude towards their response.

In summary, they seek companions who exhibit either passivity or activity in relation to the subject's fundamental attachment, commitment, gestures of affection, and concern, in order to display similar levels of passivity or activity themselves.

Passive individuals who are mutually dependent

Primarily driven by the apprehension of evading conflicts with their partners, passive co-dependents actively seek out partners whom they can mistreat, covertly allure, and manipulate into entering a relationship, fostering intimacy, or exploiting their vulnerability. They exhibit a passive demeanor when it comes to their prominent control over the subordinate, while concurrently maintaining a passive emotional connection with the unreciprocating partner.

Active co-dependents

These individuals who rely on each other are forthright and vociferous in expressing their needs to their respective partners. They insist upon being treated with respect, care, and affection, employing diverse emotional tactics for manipulation, despite the partner's persistent lack of reciprocation.

Below is a comprehensive listing of the diverse manifestations of co-dependent virtues found within individuals or within our immediate surroundings. This statement is not intended to induce alarm or anxiety, but rather to provide a cogent depiction of the prevalence of co-dependency within individuals, whether individually or collectively.

1) Caregivers: This individual exhibits nurturing tendencies towards their partner and strives to provide optimal care for their non-reciprocal counterparts. These individuals who are interdependent derive satisfaction from fulfilling their partner's expectations and commands, thereby providing complete gratification by adopting a subservient

role or exhibiting masochistic tendencies. They have developed a strong inclination towards bestowing affection and rely on love as an essential prerequisite for their existence. They attain tranquility in existence solely by embodying the roles of nurturer, caregiver, mother/father, or aide, in any capacity they so choose.

2) Romantics: These individuals who exhibit co-dependent tendencies select their partners via a sophisticated method of seeking perpetual love, romance, and enjoyment in life. These classifications of co-dependents prioritize engaging in a partnership that fosters their romantic existence or affiliation, as well as addressing their addiction or concerns surrounding intimacy. They achieve inner tranquility solely by attaining affection, validation, or even the recognition of love from another individual. This pertains to the

individual diagnosed with nymphomania, whose relationships are characterized by the cause-and-effect nature of sexual activity. He may continue to be a wanderer, while you collect various wedding bands.

3) Rescuers: This cohort of individuals with co-dependent tendencies seek fulfillment in their lives by selecting partners who are helpless addicts, unemployed, homeless, or disabled. Their tranquility can only be attained through their role as the rescuers. They experience a sense of productivity, happiness, and satisfaction solely through their role as a steadfast savior, thus dedicating themselves to supporting and actualizing the aspirations of others, consistently progressing to aid individuals in achieving their own dreams!

4) Narcissist: When the boundaries dissolve and deteriorate, an impassioned

individual with a codependent nature perceives others as being either in favor of or against their personal utility. This behavior reflects a notable lack of social engagement and a disregard for societal norms, indicating a genuine manifestation of narcissistic tendencies.

5) Victim Mentality: Another manifestation of co-dependency is the tendency to adopt a victim mindset. As previously indicated, the adoption of a victim mindset instills within an individual a perception of themselves as constantly being victimized, thereby requiring an abusive and demotivating partner as a means to find satisfaction within their own being. They experience a persistent sense of being neglected and lacking engagement as a result of victimization.

6) Linguistic impairment: An equally crucial interdependent element is the linguistic impairment. In essence, this

delineates the nature of deficient communication abilities. A decline in communication between two individuals can lead to the development of perceived connection, resulting in adverse effects on the relationship that the individual appears to derive solace and convenience from.

7) Perfectionists: Another group of individuals exhibiting co-dependent tendencies comprises those who have a strong inclination towards perfectionism. This particular group of individuals derives tranquility from the act of organizing objects, individuals, and their thoughts with meticulous precision. They are required to consistently coordinate individuals and establish their movement according to a specific methodology that they deem to be the epitome of perfection. Perfectionist individuals who are co-dependents tend to seek out partners

who hold them in high regard and admire their narcissistic traits, in order to cultivate a connection that revolves around the partner's adoration and love, thereby establishing an environment that aligns with the individual's pursuit of perfection.

8) Individuals with low self-esteem: This group of co-dependents consists of individuals who have exceptionally low levels of self-esteem. This represents a character imbued with the disposition of victimhood, as well as a profound sense of hopelessness, despair, and trepidation. These individuals with co-dependent tendencies exhibit an inclination towards partners who elicit feelings of ingratitude, inadequacy, anxiety, and concern over the perceptions held by others regarding themselves. This phenomenon can be attributed to inadequate communication abilities within the context of a

relationship, leading to a state of codependency, subsequently resulting in diminished self-esteem and overall dysfunction.

9) Inadequate Responsiveness, Reaction, and Reflexes: This aspect of codependency pertains to the deficiency in one's ability to establish appropriate boundaries with others and oneself, resulting in insufficient responsiveness, reaction, and reflexes. The presence of compromised, distorted, obscured, arduous, harmful, and unfavorable aspects in the realm of personal connections can lead to detrimental co-dependency, thereby inducing a persistent state of inadequate reactions and responses towards various stimuli, individuals, and circumstances.

10) Inadequate Reliance or Substance Abuse: Another facet of co-dependency pertains to the individual gripped by apprehension or paranoia. This

individual exhibits an intense fear of being devoid of romantic entanglements or experiencing solitude. Additionally, this reliance is contingent upon their persistent sense of entrapment, confinement, or restriction resulting from their addictive behaviors. Poorly defined boundaries of reliance and other excessive dependencies can lead to numerous insurmountable challenges regarding the attainment of independence or fostering a sense of self-contentment through isolation.

Indicators Of Interacting With An Individual Displaying Narcissistic Traits

If you harbor suspicions regarding the possibility of being involved with an individual displaying covert narcissistic tendencies, or in the event that you suspect your former partner possessed such characteristics, and are only now recognizing that you endured emotional mistreatment throughout the duration of the relationship, this particular chapter has been tailored to address your circumstances. Within this chapter, I shall guide you through eleven indications of clandestine narcissism, thereby providing you with eleven discernible means of identifying an individual who exhibits covert narcissistic traits.

If you possess suspicions regarding your interactions with, or recent encounters with, an individual exhibiting covert narcissistic behavior, the current content will provide you with guidance to discern the accuracy of your assessment.

One of the notable hazards associated with covert narcissism lies in the fact that the abuse frequently manifests in subtle ways, rendering it arduous to ascertain. However, it continues to exert an influence on one's emotional state and overall well-being, particularly when prolonged over an extended duration.

Similar to their counterparts, covert narcissists possess a pronounced sense of grandiosity and entitlement. However, what sets them apart and renders their presence more difficult to detect is the fact that covert narcissists are capable of outwardly displaying a sense of insecurity.

I would like to draw attention to a particular matter, which is that despite numerous assertions by individuals that they possess wicked and devoid natures, I must counter by stating otherwise. As these individuals are indeed human, it is inevitable that there will be an array of variations in their personalities, approaches to abuse, and even certain characteristics.

While it is possible that you may fail to recognize all eleven indicators listed here, identifying at least seven manifestations should suffice to indicate that this individual engages in abusive behavior, necessitating your immediate separation from them.

The initial indication that you are encountering an individual exhibiting covert narcissistic tendencies. One will observe the presence of a phase characterized by an excessive show of affection, as commonly referred to as love bombing. They exhibit a determined and swift approach due to their profound emotional experience.

They experience a sense of connection with you, perceiving you as an ideal partner and expressing admiration towards you at present, which elicits a tremendously gratifying sensation within you. Certainly, it is difficult to fathom who would not desire such an opportunity, wouldn't you agree?

However, the issue with individuals who exhibit covert narcissistic traits is that their behavior inevitably escalates into abusive patterns as time progresses. If you are in the company of an individual who tends to express their affection by hastily uttering the phrase 'I love you'. Approximately two to four weeks following the initial date, during a period of getting acquainted with someone, they utter the phrase "I love you."

That observation leads me to conclude that there may be indications of a covert narcissist in this situation. Individuals engage in such behavior for a multitude of reasons.

It is possible that you are encountering a distinct form of personality disorder, or it could be an individual who exhibits excessive enthusiasm and lacks comprehension of love. However, such behavior is frequently observed in individuals with narcissistic tendencies.

If you enter into a romantic partnership with an individual who exhibits an intense desire for rapid progression, and you have legitimate concerns regarding their potential narcissistic tendencies, it is not imperative for you to immediately terminate the relationship. Instead, I recommend exercising caution by slowing down the pace until you have the opportunity to observe for additional indications. If through careful observation you discern that the accelerated pace was the only cause for concern, then it would be safe to proceed.

But it's often not. When an individual exhibits a strong inclination to swiftly establish a rapport with you, typically the circumstances are unfavorable.

The second point elucidates a tendency for individuals to withhold acknowledgment of certain aspects when they find themselves captivated by an intense infatuation. During this initial phase characterized by excessive affection and admiration, individuals often experience a heightened sense of self, perceiving their romantic interest as extraordinary.

However, I am aware and I have been informed by numerous survivors who have later confessed that they sensed some peculiarities within their situations. This could simply be an intuitive feeling, as if their instincts were indicating that something was amiss.

At that juncture, one may not possess a definitive awareness of the unfavorable nature of the situation, however, usually, a sense of unease typically indicates an underlying issue. It is conceivable that their countenance betrays an indication, or perhaps they respond to specific stimuli in a discernible manner.

This diverges from any prior experiences one may have encountered, as their reactions defy typical expectations, leading to a sense of surprise and curiosity. Such behavior could potentially indicate the presence of a covert narcissistic individual.

There appears to be a slight discrepancy in their behavior. This should be considered a significant warning sign, prompting us to proceed with the subsequent steps to evaluate whether the individual in question may display these traits.

Number three can be associated with number two, albeit, number three symbolizes the cognitive dissonance encountered in the presence of this individual. This elucidates the internal dynamics that transpire when one's words and actions fail to synchronize.

You are presented with a decision to be made. You can have confidence in your own judgment, in the consistency of your actions, and in your intuition. Alternatively, you can bestow trust in someone's spoken words and the narrative they present. However, as we progress in relationships, we often encounter a stage where we discern a disparity between actions and words. It becomes apparent that there are noticeable inconsistencies, such as promises being unfulfilled or declarations of love not being reflected in behavior. When actions and words no longer align, it is at this juncture that we typically find ourselves further along in the relationship.

The fourth characteristic, indicative of narcissism, manifests as an intense desire for victory. However, regarding covert narcissists, I must assert that their true nature is often not readily apparent, contrary to what one might assume.

It is possible that you harbor preconceived notions about how a narcissist appears, and this individual would adamantly refuse to acknowledge any wrongdoing.

Well, that's not true. Envision an individual traversing the entirety of their existence without ever issuing an apology. Without ever acknowledging their own fallibility. They would not make significant progress, would they?

There are occasions when they are obliged to undertake such actions. They have committed a transgression within the framework of our societal norms, and in accordance with our principles of human rights, they must adhere to the rules and regulations of our community to an extent. Hence, there is a possibility that an apology may be extended to you by the individual exhibiting narcissistic tendencies.

The distinction between an apology extended by a narcissist and an apology offered by another individual lies in the likelihood of sincerity. Whereas someone else's apology may genuinely express remorse for causing emotional distress and induce a commitment to change their actions, a narcissist's apology is characterized by a consistent pattern of repeating the hurtful behavior, as their remorse is insincere. Over time, one will observe the narcissist's recurring inclination to prioritize their own triumph, even in inconsequential disputes.

It is possible that the individual in question is plainly incorrect, despite the presence of evidence disproving their assertions. However, they adeptly manipulate the facts in a convincing manner that portrays them as being correct. In light of this, one cannot help but ponder the motive behind expending such considerable effort for a matter of trivial significance. Why not simply acknowledge your error? However, it is inherent to the disorder.

They lack the capacity to recognize their own fallacies as acknowledging their errors would entail conceding imperfection and forsaking their grandiosity and uniqueness. It poses a formidable challenge for individuals with narcissistic tendencies to perceive the situation objectively and accurately.

In position number five, the covert narcissist displays remarkable proficiency in rationalizing their negative actions. A covert narcissist may offer a justifiable rationale when disclosing their past infidelity in a relationship.

They took action as a direct result of X. Y. And Z. They were indeed correct in relation to engaging in infidelity within their relationship.

If one observes that, in each instance wherein this individual is narrating an anecdote, there arises a sense of disagreement or apprehension regarding their decision-making. However, it appears that this individual was devoid of alternatives when faced with the moral dilemma. It is plausible that they exhibit traits consistent with covert narcissism, as they possess adeptness in rationalizing their unethical conduct.

The sixth numeral returns to your possession. How do you experience your emotions during your interactions with this individual? Has this dynamic undergone a transformation within your relationship, leading to a decreased level of comfort compared to the initial stages?

During the initial phase, commonly referred to as love bombing, you will experience a remarkable sense of exhilaration. However, once the subsequent devaluation stage unfolds, you may encounter instances where the individual subtly scrutinizes and utters remarks that undermine your self-esteem. Despite the subtlety, these sentiments may trigger a profound emotional response within you.

The unfolding sequence of events entails individuals initially harboring a profound admiration for you, perceiving you as exceptional. However, as they gradually become more acquainted with your true nature, the realization dawns upon them that you are merely mortal, possessing imperfections akin to any ordinary individual. Alas, this revelation proves intolerable for a narcissistic individual.

According to their perspective, they expect someone who possesses complete perfection, and thus when they observe your imperfections. Their sole sustenance lies in your imperfections, and despite their silence on the matter, they refrain from discussing the source of their grievances. They endeavor to induce negative emotions through surreptitious means.

They are not explicitly highlighting it; however, it is inevitable that the issue will arise. They will convey this information through various means, including verbal communication or subtle expressions conveyed through their gaze. It typically involves a confluence of factors in individuals exhibiting covert narcissistic tendencies. The act of mistreatment can manifest itself in intricately nuanced ways, which significantly complicates its detection. Therefore, I strongly advocate for individuals to observe and evaluate their emotional experiences within the context of the relationship, if they possess the ability to discern those occurrences.

It is highly probable that if being in the presence of this individual leads to a heightened sense of self-deterioration compared to the initial stages of the relationship, one may be facing emotional abuse inflicted by a concealed narcissistic individual. The specific medical prognosis may hold limited significance, as the crucial issue at hand is the emotional maltreatment endured. It is imperative that you proactively commence the process of creating emotional distance from this individual.

The seventh point pertains to the potential occurrence of noticeable manifestations of discordant fury or indignation. In the midst of a seemingly ordinary discourse, one may encounter a situation where an individual unexpectedly becomes highly agitated and reactive. This phenomenon is prevalent among individuals who exhibit covert narcissistic tendencies.

However, regarding covert narcissists, it is important to note that they are individuals who harbor deep feelings of insecurity. Nonetheless, they have an inherent need to maintain a facade in order to preserve their image. It is imperative for them to be convinced of their exceptional qualities, and it is incumbent upon you to validate and reinforce these beliefs in them. If one inadvertently touches upon a particularly sensitive aspect of a person's self-perception, an element deeply ingrained in their constructed identity, and unknowingly undermines it, it has the potential to provoke an intense reaction from them, characterized by narcissistic fury. Invariably, one may find themselves bewildered and questioning the events that transpired.

Regrettably, what started off as a lighthearted exchange between us has now resulted in a disagreement. However, I must express that I failed to communicate anything egregiously offensive during our interaction. The reason behind this individual's negative reaction is rooted in the fact that your statement undermined their self-perception, which we are aware to be unfounded.

It can be immensely agonizing for individuals with narcissistic tendencies when they are unable to momentarily perceive their own flaws. Consequently, they are prone to reacting vehemently to seemingly insignificant matters such as this.

If you have had the experience of being in a relationship with a covert narcissist, number eight is likely a familiar concept to you. That is gaslighting. Not only does it have the potential to encompass various aspects beyond cheating, but within the context of a romantic relationship, gaslighting frequently revolves around instances of infidelity.

.

In the event that the individual displaying narcissistic traits engages in infidelity, one may experience an intuitive sense of dissonance regarding the situation at hand, or conceivably possess substantial evidence suggesting that this person has indeed been unfaithful. Armed with either this intuition, concrete proof, or any relevant substantiation, it is then necessary to address the matter with the individual in question.

That individual, characterized as a narcissist, who is engaging in deception, is prone to react explosively and shift blame onto you. They may even level allegations of cheating against you, or simply make accusations of irrationality. They are attempting to manipulate you in order to divert your attention away from the subject matter.

If you were to adhere to that line of thinking and succumb to the emotional entrapment therein, you may find yourself experiencing a sense of bewilderment, akin to a momentary pause for contemplation. What just happened here? I had certain matters upon which I desired to deliberate, yet unexpectedly this individual precipitated a circumstance wherein I find myself compelled to vindicate my position.

"What just happened?"

This clearly indicates the presence of an individual who engages in emotional abuse, potentially displaying characteristics synonymous with a covert narcissist.

A subset of the aforementioned discussions pertained to general traits commonly associated with emotionally manipulative individuals, while the concluding topics on this agenda presented distinct indicators indicative of a personality disorder. However, I aim to provide you with several approaches through which you may discern the manifestation of narcissistic personality disorder in your relationship, as this holds utmost importance in determining whether you are dealing with an individual afflicted with narcissistic personality disorder rather than someone merely exhibiting self-absorption.

In either case, this distresses the individual and constitutes a grave form of mistreatment.

The ninth point pertains to a conspicuous absence of emotional empathy, which can be defined as the ability to discern and share the sentiments of others. Neurotypical individuals have the capacity to perceive and experience the emotions of others to a certain degree.

If you happen to be in the presence of an individual who is experiencing sadness, you can establish a connection or understanding.

It is intrinsic for the majority of individuals, however those with narcissistic tendencies lack the capacity to empathize with others' emotions at any degree. Certain individuals who exhibit narcissistic traits may possess a degree of emotional empathy, while cognitive empathy is undoubtedly present, implying an intellectual understanding without a corresponding emotional experience.

According to Paul, men will exhibit self-centered tendencies, demonstrating an unhealthy manifestation of self-love known as narcissism.

Self-compassion diverges from self-preservation. The act of applying cream to one's skin in order to prevent cracking caused by dryness is an expression of self-preservation. The act of taking a bath is motivated by the instinct of self-preservation, as neglecting personal hygiene leaves one susceptible to illness-causing germs. However, I find it perplexing that individuals who choose not to bathe for extended periods of time, such as those living on the streets, manage to survive without succumbing to the harmful consequences of poor hygiene. Similarly, I fail to comprehend how children who consume sand in playgrounds do not experience any adverse health effects.

The narcissist harbors profound feelings of self-disdain and self-aversion, thereby delving into the paradoxical nature intrinsic to their personality. The suffering they inflict upon others is indicative of the void within their being. They lack the ability to alleviate the void within, consequently resorting to aggression towards others.

Diverse accounts exist regarding the development of narcissism, although the majority concur that its origin can be traced back to early childhood. Infants are entirely reliant upon their parents or caregivers upon birth and crying is their sole means of communication for attending to their needs. The infant vocalizes distress, prompting the parents/caregivers to swiftly attend to the child's requirements. Consequently, the child forms a perception that the parents exist solely within the confines of their role, as they are constantly present to cater to the child's needs. However, there comes a moment when we are anticipated to undergo the transformation of recognizing ourselves as autonomous individuals and concurrently granting our parents the freedom to pursue their own individual paths. Subsequently, we distance ourselves and embark on the journey of personal development, fostering independence.

Narcissism typically arises during childhood, often as a result of inadequate care or mistreatment. Therefore, the individual makes a conscious decision: given the lack of care and attention from others and the consistent maltreatment endured, it becomes preferable to construct a personal realm wherein one can reside undisturbed. Should anyone endeavor to approach, the person in question will handle the situation accordingly. It is an unconscious phenomenon. To some extent, the narcissist truly necessitates compassion and empathy, as they are an individual who has failed to fully mature. Due to their self-loathing, individuals find it impossible to embrace their authentic identity and consequently develop affection towards their distorted self-image in the form of a reflection. One of the cunning characteristics exhibited by narcissists is their talent for mirroring individuals within their vicinity. If he were to encounter you today and discovers that you are a clergyman, he will undoubtedly engage you in conversation, delving into your profound understanding of scriptural texts to glean insights. Upon encountering you in their subsequent encounter, the individual in question shall engage in a discourse whereby they shall invoke the aforementioned scriptural passages, thereby prompting you to experience a sense of mutual connection, ultimately leading to a state of admiration and approval, thereby securing their influence and favor. In the event that you inform him of your musical occupation, he will likely respond with: "Ah, I dabble a bit in keyboard playing." May I propose the notion of collaborating musically with you in the near future? Yeah, he will reply. However, on each occasion that you attempt to rectify the situation, he will be inaccessible, as he does not possess the skill to play the keyboard, and instead provided false information to deceive you. They emulate every individual they encounter. When initially encountering a narcissist, upon perceiving qualities in you that they find valuable for enhancing their own lives, they pursue you and express the desire for a romantic relationship by stating, 'I would like you to be my girlfriend.' This phenomenon is commonly referred to as love bombing. Their ability to experience feelings of affection rapidly and unexpectedly is truly astonishing. Within a span of approximately one to two months subsequent to acquainting oneself with an individual, they may express their intention to enter into matrimony. Quickly. In relationships, it is advised to exercise caution and take a moment to reconsider when encountering individuals who exhibit a hasty or impatient demeanor towards you. They are eager to capture and entangle you in their life, in order to prevent your escape from them.

And guess what? The narcissist consistently directs their attention towards individuals characterized as empaths, who possess compassionate and empathetic qualities, as they are aware that engaging with another narcissist will yield unfavourable outcomes. Such an approach would prove futile. In numerous instances, it is often found that individuals exhibiting narcissistic traits are frequently wedded to individuals who possess exceptionally amiable dispositions. I want to clarify that both male and female individuals can exhibit narcissistic tendencies. Female individuals with narcissistic traits tend to exert a greater degree of disruptive influence, as their presence as narcissists contradicts societal norms and expectations for women. Nonetheless, it is important to acknowledge that narcissistic females do indeed exist.

Consequently, you are coerced into the relationship, leaving little room for contemplation; expeditiously, they proceed to wed you.

As you engage in the act of reading, certain realizations may begin to arise within your consciousness regarding your own being, and/or the dynamics of your interpersonal connections. The narcissist obtains the essential fuel, commonly referred to as narcissistic supply, by creating a false facade through which they appear to understand and reflect your identity. They have an intense desire for that provision, akin to the fuel one inserts into a vehicle to ignite its function and facilitate movement. The phrase 'narcissistic supply' pertains to anything that satisfies the demands of the narcissist's defenses, regardless of whether it is a primary or secondary means of nourishment. Allow me to elucidate the meaning of these two terms.

The narcissist will derive energy from the individuals in their vicinity. He is able to extract fuel from the traffic warden. Allow him to proceed by driving past, and upon being greeted or acknowledged by the warden, his fuel supply is promptly replenished. This interaction serves as a secondary means of provision, as the connection between them is somewhat distant. He has the ability to elicit input from individuals within his workplace, including the janitor, the courier, and the security personnel. He is the individual capable of discreetly distributing small amounts of money to the junior staff, leading to their subsequent admiration and reverence whenever he enters the office. He is not motivated by altruism, compassion, or kindness; rather, his actions stem from a desire to extract something from them.

The principal source is the individual who shares a direct connection with the narcissist. This individual harbors strong desire for the acquisition of this resource. The main source is prohibited from escaping the narcissist. In the event that a partner chooses to disengage from the narcissist, it is plausible for the latter to pursue the individual with intent to commit homicide or inflict grievous harm by means of acid attack. The sentiment expressed is one of possessiveness, adhering to the belief that if oneself cannot possess you, nobody else should either. You are my source of sustenance, thus it is unjust for you to unilaterally dispose of or abandon me. It is expected of you to remain in this location until the end of your life. For individuals with narcissistic tendencies, this commitment persists even after a divorce, not due to the sanctity of marriage, but due to the belief that "I will not release you until I bring about your demise." These individuals refuse to let go or release their grip on the person involved.

If you have been involved in a prior relationship from which you have withdrawn, yet the individual in question persists in causing distress and intruding upon your life, it is imperative to seek assistance from law enforcement authorities. Your life may be endangered by their unwillingness to release you. Certain individuals who lost their lives were the unfortunate victims of this causative factor. Narcissists don't let go.

Allow me to provide some insights regarding the fuel. If they are unable to acquire the necessary fuel, it is akin to the disintegration of the internal framework they have painstakingly built. So, it is imperative for them to promptly acquire fuel from any available source. The fuels possess varied ratings or levels of quality. When visiting a fuel station, one can usually find advertisements for both leaded and unleaded fuel options. Leaded fuel is priced at a lower cost compared to unleaded fuel. The narcissist is keen on categorizing their sources of validation. The efficacy of the fuel obtained from the secondary source is limited, thus it will yield negligible benefits for him. However, the most potent form of criticism he receives comes directly from the primary source, hence it is the one he inflicts the greatest degree of harm upon. The quality of fuel derived from kindness is of a lower grade compared to that obtained from unkindness. As an illustration, if he were to arise in the morning and attire himself in a refined manner, and his spouse were to remark to him,

Your appearance is quite impressive today.

He receives minimal positive reinforcement, meriting a low rating in terms of value. Let us assign it a numerical value of 10. He was only given a meager 10 units of fuel as a token of appreciation. Nevertheless, those 10 units were acquired through the laborious act of adorning oneself, an endeavor he prefers to forgo. The fuel derived from sentiments of pain, shame, frustration, or anger possesses a numerical worth of 40, representing a value threefold greater than that of the positive fuel. Therefore, he muses inwardly:

Why would I settle for 10 if it is feasible to obtain 40 from the same event? I would like to acquire the 40-inch model."

What is his occupation?" or "What is his profession? When she expresses that you appear attractive, he would respond Yes, your observation comes quite late considering our five years of marriage.

Instantly, the countenance of the spouse will undergo a transformation, signaling their acknowledgement of causing harm to the individual. He has successfully retrieved his weapon cache of 40 units. Although it appears to be a casual discussion taking place, there exists an underlying occurrence of greater significance.

I perused a published account detailing the experiences of a lady who meticulously documented her existence while entwined in matrimony with an individual displaying narcissistic tendencies. According to her, upon meeting him, he expressed his desire for marriage while also emphasizing his preference to refrain from sexual intimacy before marriage, as he wished to approach that aspect of their relationship with patience and caution. She perceived this as an act of kindness and decency on his part. They did not adhere to the Christian faith, thus when he proposed for her to cohabit with him and she sensed that their relationship was smoothly advancing, evolving, and making headway. Consequently, she cohabitated with him, yet he continues to abstain from engaging in sexual intercourse with her. After the passage of 22 years, she came to the realization that he had orchestrated a vacation for both of them, and they embarked on the journey. Two days prior to a significant occasion, he eventually engaged in a physical relationship with her, sparking a notable sense of progress. Shortly thereafter, within a span of two days, he initiated a proposal of matrimony and bestowed upon her a ring. She came to the realization that her lack of sexual involvement in the relationship posed an issue, prompting him to resolve that concern before proposing, ensuring her acceptance. Therefore, the sexual encounter can be characterized not as an expression of affection or longing, but rather as a calculated maneuver employed to entice and manipulate her. The narcissist perceives events as never occurring by mere coincidence or random occurrence. The narcissist does not leave room for coincidences as every occurrence is meticulously planned and calculated in advance. The perception of an event occurring abruptly is solely experienced by those who have been affected. It didn't. As I have increased my reading, I have observed a noticeable improvement in my ability to provide guidance within the confines of the counseling setting. There exists a strong correlation between individuals who exhibit narcissistic tendencies, those classified as psychopathic, and individuals identified as sociopathic. The narcissist, however, establishes a boundary when it comes to engaging in criminal behavior. Individuals exhibiting sociopathic and psychopathic tendencies have the propensity to engage in acts of violence, causing harm or perpetrating assaults. They display a complete absence of remorse, much like the individual with narcissistic tendencies. In formal tone: The psychopath, in contrast to the narcissist, demonstrates a greater degree of self-awareness and acknowledgment of their condition. Consequently, one can discover literature authored by psychopaths outlining the intricacies of their mindset, as well as works by sociopaths discussing their own experiences. On the other hand, there are scant offerings worldwide when it comes to narcissists writing about the complexities of their own minds, with less than five such publications known. Only one exception stands out, and this individual's motivation for writing is primarily due to their involvement in criminal activities, having been presented with the choice between imprisonment and therapeutic intervention. Naturally, he opted for therapy, and the therapist deemed it necessary for him to engage in written expression as an integral aspect of his therapeutic process. In the literary works that he authors, he espouses

Despite my prior in-depth analysis of the psychological dynamics underlying narcissistic behavior, I possess the capacity to manipulate your thoughts and emotions, should you dare to test my abilities. Certain individuals inquire as to whether I harbor concerns about divulging the entirety of the narcissist's confidential knowledge. I inform them that their extensive reading will fail to prevent me from manipulating their thoughts at will, as their cognitive capabilities are incapable of matching mine."

He has authored nearly 40 literary works, and I deeply appreciate his unique viewpoint as it facilitates comprehension. The majority of the existing literature on narcissism, approximately 95%, predominantly focuses on the perspective of the victim. However, this particular book offers an alternative viewpoint.

When engaging in this particular activity, it is justified by the underlying rationale for its execution.

This statement is made to elucidate the underlying rationale behind our use of this particular expression."

Paul refers to individuals who possess an inclination towards material wealth as "lovers of money." Narcissistic individuals rely on financial resources to bolster their sense of significance and perpetuate their facade built upon self-aggrandizement. They have placed themselves in that position, yet they require financial resources to sustain it. Financial resources enable individuals to encircle themselves with the emblems of affluence, such as extravagant automobiles, lavish residences, and luxurious apparel. The possession of wealth for the narcissist signifies a manifestation of both psychological and financial prowess, elevating them to an esteemed position wherein they are revered by all, including themselves. They have developed a dependency on receiving adulation and attention, which is facilitated by the acquisition of money. For the narcissist, money is not simply a means to an end, but rather a mechanism for exerting control. When individuals provide monetary assistance, they are driven by the expectation of receiving something in exchange, thus negating the notion of it being a genuine gift. Those individuals in authoritative positions within the workplace who utter the phrase "

Yes, I will hire you, but...you will be expected to compensate for it.

The narcissist's relationships are impacted by both their financial circumstances and their attitude towards money. For instance, it serves as a valuable asset in persuading and captivating individuals as a reservoir for potential self-centered gratification. Therefore, they do not intend to provide you with the money as a gift, but rather expect you to eventually repay it, as they will require you to furnish fuel. They will likely request certain favors from you, which may generate a sense of obligation due to their past financial contributions. It is worth noting that certain of these requested favors may occasionally involve unlawful activities. They will cause you trouble and refrain from involvement. The individuals exhibiting narcissistic behavior employ conspicuous displays of wealth as a means to obtain validation from society. Numerous philanthropists exhibit narcissistic tendencies, which frequently contributes to their heightened sense of entitlement. If you find yourself in a relationship wherein your partner consistently raises projects as soon as you come into financial means, it is quite likely that said person displays narcissistic tendencies - placing emphasis on how your money can be utilized for their benefit, rather than mutual priorities. Once it becomes apparent that you possess financial resources, individuals adeptly orchestrate a series of circumstances that will compel you to address them, ultimately depleting your monetary reserves. Do you know why? They aim to deplete your financial resources in order to establish a perpetual state of dependence on their part. Subsequently, they possess the ability to exercise their will upon you at their own discretion. These are topics that are not openly discussed within the church; however, it is noteworthy that a significant portion of the church population, approximately 10% according to statistical data, possesses this characteristic. That is huge!

www.ingramcontent.com/pod-product-compliance
Lightning Source LLC
Chambersburg PA
CBHW050416120526
44590CB00015B/1981